Life in the Valley of Death:
Some Aspects of Race in Men's Basketball
in the Missouri Valley Conference,
1959–1960 to 1963–1964

Published by Graphix Products, Inc.
399 Wegner Drive
West Chicago, IL 60185

Printed in the U.S.A.

ISBN 978-0-9749989-1-6

Library of Congress Control Number: 2007923701

Contents

Introduction

In 1891, basketball's founder, James Naismith, believed that proper hygiene and the Sermon on the Mount were more important than free throws and out-of-bounds plays. Such a viewpoint was similar to that of college football's John W. Heisman, who thought little of an award given to an individual in a team sport.[1] "Basket ball" (two words until 1921) was never a life and death issue to Naismith; he saw beyond the boys who were "compelled to throw the ball in an arc." Basketball is now enjoyed by millions throughout the world, and football has done well, too, at least in the United States.

And, once upon a time, a few young men in a remote and relatively unknown conference, the Missouri Valley, played some exciting college basketball games. The games were wonderful, not only as an exercise and a competition for the boys, but also as an entertainment for the fans, to say nothing of the possibility of yearly increase in the popularity of the sport and its concomitant profitability.

This work seeks to accomplish two things: first, to present some new details surrounding some excellent basketball play in a particular time and in some specific places, and second, to shed some theoretical light on a few black-white interactions that took place in a "backstage" that might recall Erving Goffman. Like the playing of music in a dank and dark basement among people "thrown together" there, college basketball was given to interesting racial dramas, complete with the intersection of skills, skin color, and self-presentation.

Black athletes, especially, found themselves in marginalized and liminal places, while white players did not. From the first recruiting trip to the last post-game show, the games served to produce social conditions worth serious study today.

Such a study should be unabashedly sociological, rich in the investigation of theory and theatre, two words coming from the Greeks, who desired to *see* what was being performed before them, among them, and "in them." (Was not Plato "the prophet" of seeing?) Athletic contests lend themselves easily to people seeing, actions being seen, and all sorts of visual events along the way.

This study is a commentary on some of the ways in which college basketball was racially structured between 1959 and 1964, with the hope that race as a workable concept might be done away with. Although forms and structures cannot explain everything, they may help to clarify some things in preliminary detail. A study of structures and forms has superceded gut-wrenching stories detailing the black-white struggles that have permeated American lives for so many years. Although Orlando Patterson says that a study should involve a group's "distinctive attitudes, values and predispositions,"[2] this work will articulate what certain events and features might have "looked like," maybe not so much what "really happened" from perspectives both black and white.

The section called Endnotes is extensive, and it is an open invitation for readers to do research on similar topics that are embedded in the history of college basketball and its racial affairs.

This effort presents itself in popularized form, with the hope that more serious scholars will one day come forward and research profoundly a set of social circumstances that will be at once fascinating as well as more informative.

The year 2007 marks the 100th birthday of the Missouri Valley Conference. Why not begin to study a few aspects of it with some enthusiasm?

January 12, 2007
Joliet, Illinois

CHAPTER ONE

Of Farms and Factory

The Missouri Valley Conference started as the Missouri Valley Intercollegiate Athletic Association at a meeting in the Midland Hotel in Kansas City, Missouri on January 12, 1907 involving the public universities of Kansas, Iowa, Missouri, and Nebraska, as well as (private) Washington University, located in St. Louis. (One of the representatives from Kansas was Naismith. He went 55–60 there as the head basketball coach.) A few months later Drake and Iowa State joined the group.[1]

The Missouri Valley under study here, however, consisted of seven schools in seven states. The schools were Bradley University (in Peoria, Illinois), the University of Cincinnati, Drake University (Des Moines, Iowa), North Texas State College (Denton, Texas), St. Louis University, the University of Tulsa, and the University of Wichita. The nicknames for the seven were Braves, Bearcats,

Bulldogs, Eagles, Billikens, Golden Hurricane, and Wheat Shockers respectively.[2]

The schools were situated upon a broad geography. The Valley was for the most part located in the "Middle West/South,"[3] although the case can be made today that Cincinnati might deserve three descriptions: East, Midwest, or "Foundry."[4] St. Louis can be in either the Midwest or the South; the city is where "the sugars of the South lay mingled with the cereals of the North."[5] Tulsa and Denton are more difficult to classify, since the former is in oil country (West or Southwest?), while the latter is near growing Dallas-Fort Worth, a place some would call Southwest.[6] Des Moines and Peoria are similar; both are Midwest.

The size of the schools was a different and less confusing matter, at least according to some figures from 1960. Bradley had 4,500 students. Cincinnati was not small; there were 21,038 students there. Drake, perhaps surprisingly, had 10,161 students. North Texas had 12,198. St. Louis reported 9,781. Tulsa listed 5,394. Wichita counted 5,875 students.[7]

Maybe God wanted the Valley to be successful, since several schools began under religious auspices. Bradley (1897) spoke of "chapel exercises" the year the school was started, and Cincinnati (1819) used "the Holy Protestant version" of the Bible from the first day in order to focus properly both students and teachers. Drake (1881) was started by the Disciples of Christ.[8] North Texas (1890) may not have been as religious; it was founded as a private college called Texas Normal College and Teachers' Training Institute. St. Louis (1818) is the second oldest Catholic university in the country. Tulsa, as Kendall College originally (1894), had

Presbyterian beginnings. Wichita (1895) was started by the Congregational Church as Fairmount College.

A small town/big city dynamic was at work, too.[9] St. Louis (750,026) and Cincinnati (502,550) were big in population by anyone's definition. Des Moines (208,982), Tulsa (261,685), and Wichita (254,698) were probably big to some people, but small to others. The small(er) places were Peoria (103,162) and Denton (26,844).[10]

Travel to and from the games in the Valley would have challenged Meriwether Lewis and William Clark. The longest trip was between Cincinnati and Denton, a whopping 950 miles by road; the shortest was between either Tulsa and Wichita, or Peoria and St. Louis, both routes extending approximately 170 miles one way. The distance by car from Des Moines to Wichita stretched approximately 390 miles. St. Louis to Denton was 660 miles. Tulsa to Cincinnati extended a mere 745 miles.[11]

The seven schools existed not far from some public universities ("state schools") in each of the seven states involved, but there were some significant differences. The public universities (of the Big Ten, Big Eight, and Southwest Conferences) often dwarfed the Valley schools in student populations, although the state schools were located in cities and towns that were smaller in population than the Valley locations. For example, the University of Kansas of the old Big Eight Conference (today's Big 12 [or XII]) was (and still is) located in Lawrence, Kansas (pop. 32,858), a place much smaller in population than Wichita, home to Wichita State.[12] Kansas has, however, a perennially larger student body than does Wichita. In the Big Ten, the University of Iowa drew

bigger crowds to its men's basketball games than did Drake
(owing to a larger enrollment, to be sure), although Drake (with
far fewer students) was located in larger Des Moines. Ditto for
the University of Missouri (also of the old Big Eight and today's
Big 12; located in Columbia), when placing it next to St. Louis
University. The same situation applied for the two schools to the
south: Tulsa operated near two Big Eight Conference schools, that
is in the shadows of both Oklahoma State (in Stillwater) and
Oklahoma (in Norman).[13] Both Oklahoma and Oklahoma State
were larger in student population than the University of Tulsa,
but the towns of Stillwater and Norman were individually not
larger than the city of Tulsa.

This "formula" (big cities-smaller enrollments in the Valley,
small towns-larger enrollments in the Big Ten, Big Eight, and
Southwest Conferences) becomes jostled a bit when one realizes
that Denton is not at all a bigger place in population than Austin.

The big city-small town distinction brought with it two
differing sociologies. Valley locations, with the possible exception
again of Denton, housed people of practically every stripe, while
many locales of the Big Ten and the other two conferences did
not. Peoria was more "multicultural," to use today's word, than
Champaign-Urbana, home to the University of Illinois. Des
Moines was not really on the cutting edge for diversity, but
compared to tranquil Iowa City it may have been. Gritty
Cincinnati seemed more varied than Columbus. Tulsa might have
seemed "big time" with all its virtues and problems next to
Stillwater or Norman. St. Louis was infinitely more varied than
Columbia to its west. Wichita, complete with people labeled

Mexican (later Hispanic, now Latino), was awash with flavor compared to Lawrence or Manhattan, home to Kansas and Kansas State respectively.

The Valley institutions were not "football schools" on a grand scale at all, and only a few of the schools had a vast commitment to the game, to be kind. Tulsa (26–25–0 over the period), North Texas (18–27–3), Cincinnati (23–27–0), and Wichita (30–20–0) tried their best, and on occasion won a big game or two, but clearly Bradley, Drake, and St. Louis did not devote themselves to football in the same way. Bradley played only Drake from the Valley, and the Braves went a dismal 0–5 against Butler University, 3–2 against Wabash College, and 1–4 against Wheaton College during the period. Meanwhile, Drake (27–19) had its hands full against small Idaho State both in 1962 and in 1963, not to mention against "mighty" Western Illinois in 1963 and 1964. St. Louis was bragging that it had invented the forward pass in 1906, but was playing only "club football" during the period mentioned here.

A random look at some scores may be more convincing. Iowa State mauled Drake, 46-0, in 1960. Oklahoma State was an insufficient 16–33–0 during the five-season period, but was 5–3 against the Valley, including a 1960 handling of Tulsa in Tulsa, 28–7. Wichita had to huff and puff in 1961 to beat West Texas A&M, 41–34. (The Shockers did not play strong Kansas [30–17–3] or weak Kansas State [8–41–0].) Wichita was well off to beat Hardin-Simmons, 13–6, in 1962. On that very day (September 29, 1962) powerful Arkansas (41–13–0) mauled Valley member Tulsa, 42–14. Cincinnati was wise to have avoided

Ohio State (33–10–2) in 1961; the Buckeyes were destroying hated Michigan, 50–20, about eight weeks after the Bearcats struggled to hang on versus Dayton, 16–12. Also lurking in the neighborhood were powerful Oklahoma (30–20–2) and mighty Texas (47–6–2), who probably would have blasted any Valley team. To compete with the Big Ten, Big Eight, or Southwest Conference in football with any regularity years ago would have been a lot to ask of the Valley.[14]

To be sure, Valley football was so obscure years ago that one strains to find it in some publications. In 1961 Cincinnati was playing only three Valley games (against North Texas, Tulsa, and Wichita). Drake was listed among "Small Colleges" in the September 23, 1963 issue of *Sports Illustrated* amid no mention at all of Valley football as a conference.

A final remark is that the Valley played its basketball games in some interesting places. Bradley played in its on-campus Robertson Memorial Field House (cap. 8,000), a structure built out of B-29 airplane hangars.[15] Cincinnati hosted its visitors in its bland Armory Fieldhouse (8,000) and on occasion at the Cincinnati Gardens (10,400). Drake played on its campus at the Drake Field House (5,000) and away from its campus at Veterans Auditorium (10,000) in downtown Des Moines. North Texas entertained opposing teams in its cozy and loud Men's Gym (4,500). St. Louis played at the city's Kiel Auditorium (9,300), a building so down-to-earth and folksy that one writer has suggested that it would have been a perfect place for a professional wrestling hall of fame![16] Tulsa used the county's Fairground Pavilion (7,100), in which the odor of dirt and dust competed with the smell of popcorn. Fans occasionally spotted birds flying inside the building! Wichita hosted visitors, for the most part rudely, in its "Roundhouse," also known as Levitt Arena (10,656). Fancy buildings, they were not, and they were indeed hostile to visiting teams.

Regardless of geographic, religious, or demographic template, the seven schools came to exist in a very harmonious alignment in the summer of 1957. Bradley had returned to the Valley in the 1955–1956 season, as did Drake in 1956–1957. They were joined by newly-arrived Cincinnati and North Texas for the 1957–1958 season, the same season that Detroit and Oklahoma State dropped out. St. Louis, Tulsa, and Wichita were on the spot waiting, ready to compete.

In the fall of 1957 a young man from Indianapolis, Oscar Robertson, was a sophomore at Cincinnati. In the spring of 1958 Cincinnati was the Valley champion and went to the National Collegiate Athletic Association (NCAA) tournament, where it lost to Kansas State. Kentucky won the NCAA title.

In the fall of 1958 was there anyone who could dethrone Cincinnati in the Valley? No. The team went to the NCAA tournament in the spring of 1959, but was defeated by California, who put aside the West Virginia Mountaineers for the NCAA title.

Let us now take a longer look at things; the best is yet to come.

CHAPTER TWO

The Power Increases, 1958–1960

The Valley's brilliance begins to take shape as the 1958–1959 season ends, and the winds of change are blowing from Cincinnati to Des Moines.[1] Cincinnati coach George Smith was preparing to work one more year as the varsity men's coach after having compiled a stellar record of 126–54 (.700) over the previous seven seasons. Coach Maurice John at Drake had gone 9–15 in his first season at Drake, but he was busy inserting his "system," a style of play that had produced an astounding record of 285–58 (.830) at Moberly (Missouri) Junior College. John had inherited the Drake team from John Benington, who was moving over to St. Louis from Drake. At St. Louis, Benington had taken over from Marquette University-bound Eddie Hickey, who had directed the Billikens to an impressive record of 211–89 (.703) from 1947–1948 until 1957–1958. (Hickey was truly living a great life, since he would be named Coach of the Year by the United States Basketball Writers Association [USBWA] in the spring of 1959 despite losing three of his last four games at Marquette, 23–6 overall.) Benington had arrived for the 1958–1959 season, having studied under Pete Newell at California.[2] Clarence Iba, a brother of the legendary "Mister Iba" (Henry P. Iba) at Oklahoma State, was preparing for his last year at Tulsa. Sailing along under warm Wichita skies was Ralph Miller, a respectable 128–80 (.615) up to this point since his arrival for the 1951–1952 season. To round out the field, Bradley was loaded, but North Texas was not.

Odds-on favorites Bradley and Cincinnati were planning strategy for their two upcoming collisions, and the entire Valley was indeed ready for battle at the start of the 1959–1960 season. Bradley had been an eye-popping 45–11 in the previous two seasons, and that was *before* the varsity play of incoming sophomore Chet Walker! Just the thought of Cincinnati's Oscar Robertson returning for his senior year (32.6 points and 16.3 rebounds as a junior!) was enough to terrify anyone. St. Louis boasted of 6'10" Bob Nordmann and his teammates; they had beaten the California Bears, 55–43, and St. John's, 72–63, and it was coach John Benington's *first* year on the job with a record of 20–6! Drake's Jim ("Gus") Guydon was ready to resume his steady scoring. Coach Pete Shands at North Texas resigned on October 8, 1959, and Charles Johnson was ready to try his hand at coaching the Eagles. The Valley was preparing to be extremely rough-and-tumble, both for teams within the Conference itself and for those from without who dared to take on Valley squads.

In the fall of 1959, the Cincinnati Bearcats were still smarting from a close loss to Cal, 64–58, in the semifinals of the NCAA tournament in the previous spring. Oscar Robertson had gone only five of 16 from the field in that game. Cal had advanced to face (and beat) West Virginia, 71–70, for the NCAA title. Cincinnati had been fourth best in scoring offense (86.7 points per game) in the country. Bradley had been edged by St. John's in the 1959 National Invitation Tournament (NIT) championship game in overtime, 76–71. The Bearcats had ended the season with a glowing record of 26–4, paced by Robertson, while the Braves from Bradley were 25–4, anchored by Bobby Joe Mason and Joe Billy McDade.[3]

TABLE 1 – MVC teams against one another

	1959–60	1960–61	1961–62	1962–63	1963–64
Bradley	12–2	9–3	10–3	6–6	7–5
Cinn.	13–1	10–2	11–2	11–1	6–6
Drake	4–10	7–5	6–6	3–9	10–2
N. Texas	1–13	1–11	0–12	4–8	1–11
St. Louis	9–5	7–5	5–7	6–6	6–6
Tulsa	5–9	2–10	4–8	5–7	2–10
Wichita	6–8	6–6	7–5	7–5	10–2

Table 1 reveals clearly the results of some magnificent play during the 1959–1960 season. For starters, Bradley and Cincinnati were awesome. The Braves began by winning six in a row, and then 15 in a row, sandwiched around a single loss at

Cincinnati. The Bearcats were a terror, too; they still had Oscar Robertson. St. Louis experienced a good year (19–9 overall, 9–5 MVC), defeating in the process several "big name" schools and coaches: Kentucky (Adolph Rupp) by 12 points, North Carolina (Frank McGuire) by 16, Providence (Joe Mullaney) by four, and Kansas State (Fred "Tex" Winter) by eight. And in the wings warming up was Wichita State, a quiet 14–12 overall. The Shockers were "fixin'" to go on a rampage, to be winning on average at least 18 games per season and as many as 23 games in one season between 1960–1961 and 1964–1965.

On December 1, 1959 the Valley was indeed ready. North Texas defeated West Texas by six, Drake clobbered North Dakota by 34, Cincinnati drilled Indiana State by 35, and St. Louis pummeled Abilene Christian by 25.

Meanwhile, *Sports Illustrated* acknowledged that Bradley's Walker was something special,[4] and Cincinnati served notice to Iowa in New York City at the end of December that the Bearcats would not be trifled with, trouncing the Hawkeyes, 96–83.

The year 1960 started with a bang, since on the second day John F. Kennedy announced he would run for the presidency. On that same day Bradley crushed highly regarded St. Louis, 86–64, in Peoria.

One game that stands out in the 1959–1960 season, and indeed is still talked about, was the one pitting Cincinnati (13–0 at the time) against Bradley (12–1; the lone loss at Cincinnati) on January 16, 1960 in Peoria. Bradley won, 91–90, in a thrilling game decided at the wire, but not before jaws were dropping because of the play of both Robertson and Walker. Walker registered 28 points; teammates Al Saunders and Bobby Joe Mason scored 22 and 21 respectively. The Field House was ready to explode in the closing seconds. Robertson scored 46 points, and of Walker it was written, "he could play basketball with the likes of Oscar Robertson."[5]

Come time for the NCAA tourney in 1960, the Valley was represented well by Cincinnati. The Bearcats did lose (again) to eventual NCAA runner-up Cal, 77–69, but they had demolished DePaul by 40 points and Kansas by 11 on the way to the title game with Cal. Cincinnati finished at 28–2 (13–1 MVC), third in the country. The Bearcats defeated New York University, 95–71, in Robertson's last collegiate game. He scored 32 points.

Bradley was invited to play at the end of the regular season, too. The Braves went to the NIT tourney in New York City, where the team beat Dayton, St. Bonaventure, and Providence en route to the championship. The Braves were so strong that they beat high-flying Providence for the title by 16 points, although Walker scored only nine.[6] St. Louis did make the field in the NIT, but lost to Providence, 64–53. Not one Big Ten school participated in the NIT. The Big Eight Conference and the Southwest Conference were also absent. Len Wilkens of Providence was the tournament MVP.

The message was clear: playing against the Valley, or at least against four or five teams in it, might have been a bad idea. The Valley was starting to be painful for its opponents.

Oscar Robertson ended his collegiate career in the spring of 1960 by going 79–9 overall (.898) and 39–3 in the Valley. He averaged over 30 points per game for three varsity seasons. He totaled 1,338 rebounds and 2,973 points.[7] Some will recall that

Robertson once torched St. Joseph's of Philadelphia for 48 points as Cincinnati demolished the Hawks, 123–79.

The NCAA title in 1960 went to a Big Ten team, Ohio State, which finished at 25–3 overall (13–1 Big Ten). The Buckeyes won the title against powerful Cal by 20 points, 75–55, in coach Fred Taylor's second year. Star players for the "Taylor tots" were Jerry Lucas, John Havlicek, and Mel Nowell, among others. Lucas himself averaged a remarkable 26.3 points per game and 16.3 rebounds per game. (The team was 78–6 overall with him!) The Buckeyes averaged an astounding 91.6 points per game. They had defeated handily Western Kentucky, 98–79, Georgia Tech, 86–69, and New York University, 76-54, on the way to the title game against Cal. In the Cal-Cincinnati semifinal, Robertson again was defended brilliantly by Cal; he went only four out of 16 from the field. The Final Four was played west of the Mississippi at the Cow Palace in San Francisco.

The 1959–1960 season ended with Iowa State not having played Drake, Ohio State not knowing the way to Cincinnati, and neither large Kansas school (Kansas or Kansas State) finding the roads down to friendly Wichita. It may have been odd that Kansas did not play Wichita; the coach of the latter, Ralph Miller, was a graduate of the former. (He had attended some lectures at Kansas by Naismith, basketball's inventor. The youthful Miller was 22 years of age when the ministerial Naismith was 59.) Illinois, for what it is worth, bragged about Mannie Jackson of Edwardsville, Illinois, a black, as the team's captain,[8] but the team for some reason did not have Bradley, a mere 90 miles away, on its schedule.

On the national scene, a very good player was finishing up at Providence College, the previously mentioned Wilkens. He was one-half white and one-half black, although soon to be treated by the majority in his post-Providence days as if he were "only" black. Similar to Robertson in the field of Business Administration, Wilkens excelled in the classroom in Economics.

On March 3 the stars must have been in some kind of strange alignment across the land. In the National Basketball Association (NBA) the Syracuse Nationals murdered the defense-minded Boston Celtics, 149–108, and Lucille Ball filed papers for a divorce from Desi Arnaz, citing "grievous mental suffering" in the process.

The Valley was showing a more predictable side on March 3. St. Louis was preparing for an upcoming home game against despised Bradley, although fans going to Kiel Auditorium had to check the date on their tickets. On March 4 professional wrestler "Whipper" Billy Watson was scheduled to take on Gene Kiniski in a "death match"! (Miraculously, both somehow survived.) The Braves beat the Billikens on March 5, 81–71.

The fun of playing against Valley schools was just starting. The conference was a splendid 128–75 (.631) overall.

CHAPTER THREE

Bearcats Forever! 1960–1961

If the season previous to this one needed an encore, it certainly received one. What could be more incredible than a coach winning the NCAA title in his second year, like Ohio State's Fred Taylor did the previous season? A coach winning it in his first year would be special. That is exactly what Ed Jucker at Cincinnati did. And whom did Cincinnati beat? Ohio State. Like attracts like.[1]

The Bearcats started slowly, losing three of their first eight games, causing eyebrows to be raised. How could a team be 5–3 in the early going after a season of 28–2? St. Louis trounced the Bearcats by 17 and Bradley pasted them by 19. Then the losing stopped for the Bearcats. They proceeded to go the rest of the way undefeated. They tipped Ohio State in the title game, 70–65. The Buckeyes had been 27–0 up to the championship game.

Buckeye fans could not find fault with their star, Jerry Lucas. He scored 27 points and collected a dozen rebounds in the title game. With him and others in the lineup, coach Fred Taylor was an incredible 114–8 (.934!) in the years covered here, just for the record.

Stars for the Bearcats were Paul Hogue, Tom Thacker, and Tony Yates, among others. (Oscar Robertson had graduated from Cincinnati. He was playing professional basketball for the Cincinnati Royals and was averaging 30.5 points per game. He was the league's assist champion at 9.7 per game as a rookie! Some observers mistakenly think he played on this Bearcat title team. He did not.)

In the NCAA tournament, the Bearcats had put aside Texas Tech by 23, Kansas State by five, and Utah by 15 on the way to the title game. Cincinnati finished 27–3 overall and were again Valley champions (10–2). Fred Taylor of Ohio State, again for the record, had been an incredible 52–3 overall up to the title game.[2] Coach Jucker of the Bearcats became the first coach to succeed a coach (George Smith) from the same school and make it to the Final Four. Ohio State and Cincinnati became the first schools from the same state to play for the big trophy.[3] A young graduate assistant at Indiana University, Dick Enberg, helped cover the game in Kansas City. The game was televised live only in Ohio.

Bradley was very good, too. The school went 20–6 (9–3 MVC), but a theme was developing: the Braves were hitting a firm wall against the Bearcats from Cincinnati. Bradley was once again a bridesmaid. That image would haunt the team and its rooters for what seemed to be a lifetime. To make matters worse, there was no post-season play for the Braves; the team suffered "a dismal basketball campaign,"[4] to hear the school's yearbook tell it. Some teams would die to be so dismal today.

And, lo and behold, Drake was coming on strong at 19–7 (7–5 MVC). The Bulldogs split with Iowa State, won the Queen City Tournament at the foot of Main Street in Buffalo, and split with Bradley. Ironically, Drake lost to Bradley on February 12 in Des Moines, 83–77, but had beaten the Braves on January 18 in Peoria, 86–76, snapping a 46-game Bradley winning streak there. The Bulldogs were ranked number 14 in the country on January 3, 1961. On February 28, Drake was edged by Coach Eddie Hickey and his Marquette Warriors, 74–72, in Milwaukee, as the new Marquette mascot, "Willie Wampum," made his debut.[5]

The days in St. Louis were not bad, either. The team was 7–5 in the Valley. John Benington's Billikens defeated Iowa by six in Iowa City, Cal by one "out there," Kentucky by two in Lexington no less, St. John's by three at Kiel Auditorium in St. Louis, and Notre Dame by 14 in South Bend. The Billikens advanced to the NIT final game, bowing to Joe Mullaney's Providence Friars, 62–59, at Madison Square Garden. (In the semifinal game of the NIT there was a very unusual play: Vinnie Ernst of Providence sank a free throw against Holy Cross near the end of the game, but the ball came back out of the basket due to Holy Cross students shaking the backboard! Providence won anyway, 90–83.[6])

Coach Mullaney of Providence had good luck against the Valley. He was 3–0 against Benington and St. Louis in three attempts in the NIT (1959, 1960, 1961) and 5–1 against

Benington in the five-year period. Excessive partying in Providence after the 1961 NIT championship win caused Providence College President Rev. Robert J. Slavin, O.P., to remark, "Seven hundred years of Dominican scholarship, and nobody ever heard of us until we put five kids on the floor at Madison Square Garden."[7]

The streets of St. Louis had to be buzzing: the baseball Cardinals were coming off a good season (86–68; 1,096,632 in attendance at faltering Sportsman's Park), to say nothing of professional bowler and local favorite Dick Weber being named national kegler of the year. The pro basketball team in town, the Hawks, anchored by Bob Pettit and Cliff Hagan, were successful, too, going 51–28 in the regular season.

Wichita, for its part, accumulated a record of 18–8 (6–6 MVC) and went 3–0 at the All-College Tournament in Oklahoma City in December. There was no post-season play for the Shockers, however. Today a team with a record of 18–8 would be grabbed by the NIT selection committee, and possibly by the NCAA, in no time.

Once again, there were no Big Ten, no Big Eight, and no Southwest Conference teams participating in the NIT at all.

The recruitment of players, the absolute lifeblood of the college game, was continuing apace with the excellent records of the Valley teams. A very big name was coming aboard at Wichita, Dave Stallworth. Another name arriving on the scene was that of Levern Tart at Bradley. Marv Torrence was showing that he could play at Drake; he averaged 11.4 rebounds per game in the 1960–1961 season. The cupboard was full.

The seven teams in the Valley were a good 116–71 (.620) overall during this particular season, and more trouble for opponents was only a bounce pass away, from the top of the key to either side of the foul line extended. The Valley was 74–29 (.718) against non-conference teams.

Probably convinced of the Valley's dominance was A. E. "Abe" Lemons, the coach at Oklahoma City University, who went 3–4 against the Valley during the 1960–1961 season. His teams were defeated twice by Wichita, once by Tulsa, and once by St. Louis. OCU did manage to beat the two weaker teams, North Texas twice and Tulsa once. It is a good thing that Cincinnati, Drake, and Bradley did not take on OCU.[8] Things would have been worse for Abe's Indians. (Creighton University in Omaha played the Valley sparingly, and was a bit weary for it, too. The Blue Jays went 0–5 in the years covered here.)

The big news in Denton was a change of name. North Texas State College became North Texas State University as of August 29, 1961. Little news surrounded the men's basketball team.

Behind the scenes, Valley Commissioner Norvall Neve was a busy beaver. His office (suite 205, President Hotel, Kansas City, Missouri) was attempting to get Louisville, Marquette, and Memphis State (Memphis now) to join the Valley, and Detroit to come back to the league. In that process Director of Athletics E. W. Lambert of Memphis informed Marquette Athletic Director Laurence A. ("Moon") Mullins, "Our present plans are to house all visiting teams with colored personnel at the Naval Base in Millington, a suburb of Memphis."[9] Lambert also wrote of the desire of North Texas administrators to place its lone black basketball player with, in Lambert's words, "a private family" in the area.

Meanwhile, in Iowa City, the eyes of college basketball recruiters were fixed on a very tall, black player, Cornelius ("Connie") Hawkins, from Boys High in Brooklyn. An even 1,000 miles from home, he was turning heads in the gym with high-flying moves, tremendous scoring ability, and stories of dreadful poverty in the Bedford-Stuyvesant section of Brooklyn.

CHAPTER FOUR

Bearcats Again! 1961–1962

Certainly nothing could top the accomplishments of last year in the Valley. Correct? Wrong again. The Valley was back, more than ready to put a licking on foes outside of the Valley and draw national attention.

The summer of 1961 was eventful. Baseball's Roger Maris and Mickey Mantle were putting on a show to see who could break Babe Ruth's home run record; the Yankees and the Reds met in the World Series in the fall, with New York winning four games to one.[1] Rock 'n' roll, simultaneously both despised and loved, was flexing its songwriting muscles; Carole King asked, "Will You Still Love Me Tomorrow?," pushing the sexual envelope a bit. And there was some social upheaval, but not much, on September 12th when the National Aeronautics and Space Administration (NASA) decreed that women and the space program were not to be mixing.

In the world of Valley basketball, the worst-kept secret was that Bradley and Cincinnati were loaded again. The Cincinnati Bearcats would go a superb 29–2 (11–2 MVC), tied with Bradley in the Valley race. The Bearcats lost a game in Peoria to Bradley, 70–68, but turned the tables convincingly on the Braves in Cincinnati, 72–57. The only other loss for the Bearcats was to Wichita.

Bradley followed suit, and Cincinnati. The Braves went 21–7 overall, and the great Chet Walker concluded at the Hilltop with an overall record of 69–14 (.831). He was 31–8 in Valley games alone. In three years he scored 1,975 points, averaging 24.4 points and 12.8 rebounds per game. The Braves suffered a rare loss at home when the Butler University Bulldogs from Indianapolis came calling and edged the Braves, 80–77. Even though Walker scored 28 points, Butler hit on 17 of 23 shots from the floor in the second half.

Bradley and Cincinnati clashed in a playoff game in neutral Evansville, Indiana, and maybe the longer drive for the Braves (325 miles, as opposed to 215 for the Bearcats) was too much for the guys from Peoria. The Bearcats beat the Braves, 61–46. Bradley fans were exasperated; Cincinnati had won again. The game was Walker's second last. The final game for the Braves and Walker took place in the NIT. The Braves lost to Duquesne, 88–85.[2]

For St. Louis there was the need to recruit a bit better, since the Billikens were 11–15 overall and 5–7 in the Valley. They did, however, defeat some big schools, like Kansas and Iowa. (Lest one forget, the loss of the Hawkeyes to St. Louis probably was not as important in American life as Dr. Martin Luther King leading a demonstration in Albany, Georgia the same day.) Other schools that were not so big, like Notre Dame and Marquette, were beaten, too, by the Billikens. Coach Benington made sure there would be no lowering of the bar for the Billikens; he had on next year's schedule Ohio State, Kansas State, Providence, St. John's, Washington, and UCLA, *all on the road!*

The roads to and from St. Louis stretched north about 170 miles so that the Billikens and the Braves could play each other, often as the last game of the regular season and in the first week of March. Life in central Illinois pretty much stopped when the two teams played, and life in St. Louis just about did the same, unless the baseball Cardinals were doing their thing in spring training, of course. Shoes and booze took on soybeans and a deck of cards.

Drake went 16–8 overall (6–6 MVC), again winning the Queen City Tournament in Buffalo by conquering St. Joseph's of Philadelphia and Cornell. The Bulldogs found a nice winter home in Buffalo; they would win the Queen City Tournament four times in as many tries between 1960–1961 and 1967–1968. In the history of the tournament no team equaled that. That accomplishment, however, probably did not match the excitement of Drake's thrilling, one-point loss to eventual national champ Cincinnati, 60–59, in Des Moines on December 11th.

In Wichita there was optimism. The Shockers went 18–9 (7–5 MVC). They beat Purdue of the Big Ten in West Lafayette on December 11th, and Wichita's Gene Wiley registered 15 blocked shots in that game! He totaled 80 for the season.

At North Texas, people were bragging that they had their first All-MVC honorable mention player, John Savage.[3] Otherwise, winter nights were long in Denton. The Eagles defeated only three teams, Hardin-Simmons twice and Abilene Christian once, and conquered no one in the Valley. To add insult to injury, they went a full two months without a win, from late December to the same time in February. The "Flock" did not have much of a home court advantage.[4]

The real story was Cincinnati. They won the NCAA title by beating Ohio State, 71–59, for the second time in as many years. Significant players were Paul Hogue, Tom Thacker, and Tony Yates for the Bearcats, as well as John Havlicek, Jerry Lucas, and Mel Nowell for the Buckeyes. Cincinnati had beaten Creighton by 20, Colorado by 27, and UCLA by two to get to the title game. Ohio State, for its part, had defeated Western Kentucky by 20, Kentucky by ten, and Wake Forest by 16. Paul Hogue of the Bearcats was the NCAA tournament Most Outstanding Player.

The Bearcats were certainly the kings of Cincinnati, and other teams in the city (502,550 souls in 1960, and decreasing) could only dream. Baseball's Reds had been a good 98–64, although pro basketball's Royals were only 43–37, drawing an average of 4,725 fans, even with Oscar Robertson. (Hockey was in cold storage, between the departure of the Mohawks and the arrival of the Wings.) The center of the basketball universe may have been found in southwestern Ohio.

In the NIT in New York (where a program was an expensive 50 cents!), the four teams that survived were all Catholic: Dayton, St. John's, Loyola of Chicago, and Duquesne. Two Valley schools were also-rans: Bradley, which lost to Duquesne by three, and Wichita, which lost to Dayton by eight. Dayton won the NIT title over St. John's. Loyola had only four losses all year, perhaps a harbinger. Their rooters may have been thinking along with the fans of the old Brooklyn Dodgers with their chant, "Wait till next year!"

Former Valley poster child Oscar Robertson was not at the University of Cincinnati, of course, but was playing for the city's NBA team. He averaged 31 points, 12 rebounds, and 11 assists for the 1961–1962 season, only his second season in the league. To use the theological passive, hallowed was Robertson's name in Cincinnati. (For the record, his friend, Wilt Chamberlain, was averaging 50 points, 25 rebounds, and 49 minutes a game![5])

Bradley and Cincinnati could do some bragging. Both schools had five overlapping consecutive 20-win seasons starting in 1957–1958 and ending in 1961–1962. When the two played in central Illinois, life came to a halt in order to follow the game. When the two engaged in southwestern Ohio, things stopped until the game was over. Oscar Robertson never won in Peoria; Chet Walker always lost in Cincinnati. The two individuals and teams fit together on the court like hot two-way chili (over spaghetti) and cold Hamm's beer.

The year doubtless ended on a high note due to the success of the Cincinnati Bearcats, but did anyone notice that four Big Ten schools engaged Butler University (in Indianapolis, of course) on the hardwood? Illinois, Michigan, Michigan State and Purdue were the schools. If they could deal with an institution from Indianapolis, could dealing with a school in St. Louis or Des Moines present an obstacle?

Maybe some schools in the Midwest and Southwest were not exactly located at "the hither edge of free land," to borrow Frederick Jackson Turner's phrase, after all.

CHAPTER FIVE

The Game, 1962–1963

Certainly nothing could be better than two national championships in a row, unless one counts five teams winning 16 games or more, with one team of those five competing for the NCAA championship. Those things are exactly what happened in the Valley during the 1962–1963 season. Figures were glowing again.

Bradley was good again at 17–9 (6–6 MVC), although probably not good enough in the minds of the school's fan(atic)s. Nevertheless, the school's Mack Herndon was the Valley scoring champion at 22.7 points per game.

Drake experienced some good news and some bad: the overall record was an insufficient 11–14, and a paltry 1–9 on the road, but victories were recorded against Indiana, Minnesota, and in-conference foe Bradley.

Tulsa (5–7 MVC, but 17–8 overall) was very good with Jim King and Gary Hevelone. The Golden Hurricane beat Purdue and swept Arkansas. King by himself was, in Oklahoma terms, "all man and a yard wide" on the basketball court. Coach Joe Swank at Tulsa was walking tall.

An important doubleheader took place at the Chicago Stadium on January 26th. Cincinnati took on Illinois and beat them 62–53, while Loyola of Chicago opposed a good Santa Clara team, conquering them, 82–72. In the stands there was some speculation: what would it be like if Loyola took on Cincinnati? Time would tell.

A few weeks before the Chicago doubleheader the St. Louis Billikens had administered a relentless and terrible beating on none other than Adolph Rupp and his Kentucky Wildcats, 87–63, at Kiel Auditorium in St. Louis. The Billikens would go an impressive 11–1 at home, losing only to in-conference rival Cincinnati.

Indeed, in these days no one was wise to play the Valley. Whether large or small, urban or rural, the schools taking on the Valley paid for it. The Conference was called "the valley of death."[1]

And there was more. Dave Stallworth of Wichita put on an incredible performance against none other than Cincinnati, tallying 46 points on February 16, 1963 in Wichita. He made 14 of 22 from the floor and 18 out of 23 from the line. The final score, incredibly, was 65–64 in favor of Wichita!

Loyola and Cincinnati were on a collision course, but some other business had to be taken care of before the NCAA tournament final. Loyola had to get past Tennessee Tech, Mississippi

State, Illinois, Duke, and then, the basketball gods willing, the Ramblers were to face the Bearcats from Cincinnati in the final game of the NCAA tournament. Loyola destroyed Tennessee Tech, 111–42, edged Mississippi State, 61–51, thumped Illinois, 79–64, and trounced Duke, 94–75. The Ramblers had warmed up on Loyola of the South, 88–53, in the regular season finale.

Texas (by five), Colorado (by 7), and Oregon State (by 24) fell before the gritty Bearcats, leading up to the showdown with Loyola.

A game of games was waiting for the championship stage on March 23, 1963 at Freedom Hall in Louisville: patient and controlled Cincinnati versus racehorse Loyola. It was Bearcat defense (53 points per game allowed) versus Rambler offense (92 points scored per game), public institution versus private (i.e., Catholic), large school versus small.

Going into the game, Ed Jucker could boast of experience: he had coached at the Merchant Marine Academy (Kings Point, New York), and at Rensselaer Polytechnic Institute (Troy, New York), and was 153–45 as a head coach at Cincinnati, while George Ireland was 172–120 in twelve years at Loyola only. Quick-moving Loyola was up against "scientific" Cincinnati; James Naismith would have been proud of the patience and sense of control on the part of the Bearcats. Interestingly, at least one observer had predicted that Duke would be the one to take on the Bearcats.[2]

The game started as a dream for Cincinnati. They were leading in the early going, 19–9, and at the half, 29–21. Loyola's quick style seemed to be faltering; they missed 13 of their first 14 shots. With less then 14 minutes left, Cincinnati was comfortably ahead, 45–30, and it looked like a third straight title was going to be awarded to the Bearcats. With a lead of 15 points, and in the absence of a shot clock, they seemed to be cruising.

But things changed. Loyola's shots began to go in, and the Ramblers raced the Bearcats to the wire.[3] Without one substitute playing even a minute, Ireland's team seemed to get stronger and stronger as the game wound down. With twelve seconds left, Loyola was down by one, but Cincinnati had the ball. Jerry Harkness of Loyola fouled Larry Shingleton, who made the first free throw, making the score 54–52 in favor of the Bearcats (in the days before the 3-point field goal). Shingleton, however, missed the second free throw. Harkness scored at the other end with six seconds remaining, tying the score at 54, and overtime was next. Back in Chicago, Loyola rooters kept their ears to the radio as they heard the excited commentary of Wesley "Red" Rush. (This exciting game was not broadcast on live television in Chicago.[4]) At the very end of the overtime, a put-back by Vic Rouse provided Loyola with a thrilling win, 60–58. The victory was enjoyed by Loyola's four "tall and terrific tan shooters."[5] This trip to the NCAA tourney was Loyola's first.

Incredibly, Loyola's five starters played every minute of regulation time and overtime. No title-winning team has done that since. The box score also reveals another unbelievable thing: Loyola shot 23 out of 84 from the field, a miserable .274. (Cincinnati shot 22 out of 45 [.489].) No championship-winning team has matched Loyola's dismal shooting percentage since. The victory, and the untiring style by which it was won, may have been a reflection of Ireland, a take-no-hostages, very determined coach in his day.

The close score makes room for some theory about which team executed good and proper techniques in order to win, and which team performed as if it did not want to lose.[6] Cincinnati coach Jucker made possibly a fatal mistake thinking that choosing not to play aggressively on offense was as effective as playing good defense. Or, said differently, maybe Jucker believed that winning the game was going to reflect the axiom that defense wins championships.[7] Should not the Bearcats have played more aggressively (i.e., less patiently) on offense with a big lead?

Earlier in the day, Jucker had given a talk at the National Association of Basketball Coaches (NABC) luncheon. He said, "Anyone capable of walking on a basketball court can play good defense."[8] A more accurate wording (amid some second-guessing) might have been, "Not just anyone can execute the intricacies of offense with teammates, and players have to be patiently instructed to execute hard-to-learn details on offense better than the opposition can execute them."

The Bearcats helped the Ramblers by committing 16 turnovers, compared to only three by Loyola. Nevertheless, the Bearcats had made it to the championship game three straight years, recalling the accomplishments of Ohio State.[9] Loyola won their tournament games by an average of 23 points per game. No team has done that since, either.

Imagine the thoughts and emotions of the Wichita players at the end of the season. They had defeated both Cincinnati and Loyola! On February 16th in Wichita the Shockers beat the

Bearcats, and on March 2nd in Chicago, Wichita beat Loyola by a point before 18,778 fans. Furthermore, the Bearcats for their part saw their 37-game winning streak snapped by the Shockers in Wichita, as Dave Stallworth lit them up for 46 points. Stallworth was "held" to only 28 points against Loyola![10]

Bowling Green was the only other team to beat Loyola all year. The Falcons trounced the Ramblers, 92–75. Cincinnati lost only to Wichita and Illinois.

A very good player for Cincinnati was George Wilson, whose family had moved from Meridian, Mississippi to Chicago. He had played at Marshall High in Chicago, and was the *Chicago Sun-Times* high school player of the year in 1960. Wilson's Marshall Commandos won Illinois state titles in 1958 and 1960.[11]

In the NIT, meanwhile, St. Louis lost to Marquette, and Wichita fell before Villanova.[12] No Big Ten team was present. Schools from the Big Eight and the Southwest Conference were absent, too. Again, possibly by some divine quirk, the final four teams in the NIT were all Catholic: Providence, Canisius, Marquette, and Villanova. They replaced last year's Catholic finalists: Dayton, St. John's, Loyola, and Duquesne. The only entrant in the tourney from the "West" was the Valley's Wichita. Providence won the NIT for the second time in three years. The Friars beat the Golden Griffins of Canisius College for the title.

The Valley displayed an overall record of 116–67 (.634), which was even more glowing than the previous year's 105–83 (.559). One will never know how many teams chose not to play in the "valley of death."

Away from the Valley, observers were noticing that by early February long and tall "Connie" Hawkins was not at Iowa. He was busy playing for the Harlem Globetrotters. He had been allegedly involved with taking a bribe at Iowa. Meanwhile, a star was born in Hawkins' Brooklyn in that same month and year, a little boy named Michael Jeffrey Jordan.

Once again the streets of St. Louis were buzzing. Work began downtown on February 12th on a large arching structure that would remind everyone of the westward movement of people decades earlier. On the same day, Billikens fans were still talking of their hard-earned victory at home over Wichita a few days earlier, 68–61.

CHAPTER SIX

Great Times in Peoria, 1963–1964

In the early summer of 1963, three young "freedom riders" were killed in Mississippi, and in August Dr. Martin Luther King, Jr. gave his stirring "I Have a Dream" speech in Washington, D.C. near the Lincoln Memorial.[1] He begged that both whites and Negro people (his words) be aware of "the flames of withering injustice" and that both groups "must ever conduct our struggle on the high plane of dignity and discipline." Several months later, the dignity and discipline of all American people were severely questioned on Friday, November 22nd when President John F. Kennedy was killed in Dallas.

Although many Valley basketball fans were probably licking their chops about the upcoming season, the previous year's success in the Valley (*five* teams with 16 wins or more) doubtless looked small after the assassination. The games might have seemed to be little more than 40 minutes of trying to throw a round ball through a ring exactly twice the ball's diameter. Life moved on, although certainly with a diminished view of sports and games on all levels.[2] Dr. King watched the Kennedy funeral procession move through the streets of Washington. He was not invited to participate in any capacity.

In the Valley the "theme," if there had been one, may have had something to do with the necessity to carry on despite some ugly circumstances in the nation. Surviving well was the new sheriff in Dodge, or at least in Wichita, the Wheat Shockers. The team was paced by its Associated Press and United Press International first-team All-American, Dave Stallworth. The team went 23–6 and 10–2 in the Valley.

Cincinnati lost a home game to put an end to their 72-game home winning streak. Kansas beat them, 51–47. Worse still, the Bearcats later saw their 41-game winning streak in Valley games stopped in January by Bradley.

On February 8th the stars must have been in an advantageous alignment again. Bradley edged fourth-rated Wichita in a thriller, *American Bandstand* debuted in Hollywood (having left Philadelphia), and the Beatles were warming up for their appearance on *The Ed Sullivan Show* the next day. Talk about excitement …

Drake also went 10–2, and had to face Wichita at the end of the season in a winner-take-all playoff on a neutral court, Allen Fieldhouse, on the campus of the University of Kansas in Lawrence.[3] The Shockers edged the Bulldogs in what must have been a coach's dream, 58–50.

Wichita advanced to the NCAA tourney, beating Creighton, 84–68, but the Shockers lost to Kansas State in Wichita (of all places), 94–86. Stallworth went 14–22 from the field and 9–12 from the free throw line for 37 points. (Both Wichita and Drake found Lawrence for the playoff game, of course, but Kansas and Kansas State were apparently unable to find Wichita for a game in the regular season.)

Bradley (20–6, 7–5 MVC) was doing well. They beat Cincinnati in Cincinnati, although they lost to the Bearcats in Peoria. As the third-place team in the Valley, the Braves headed off to New York City and again won the NIT, practically making the NIT and the city a second home.[4] Braves rooters cheered wins over St. Joseph's of Philadelphia, Army, and the Lobos of New Mexico. A total of 15,137 people in New York saw Levern Tart and Bradley dominate the guys from Albuquerque in an afternoon game, 86–54.[5]

Drake at season's end was invited to the NIT and went 1–1, beating Pittsburgh, but losing to eventual finalist New Mexico. McCoy McLemore starred for Drake in the regular season, averaging 11.8 rebounds a game. He grabbed 21 in a game against St. Louis on February 29, 1964, a leap day, and he averaged 15.5 points per game to boot. Coach Maurice John was doing well in his sixth year, although his expertise would not become nationally recognized for a few more years. He was happy to pick up the 1964 Coach-of-the-Year award in the Valley.

St. Louis, meanwhile, was 6–6 in the Valley and 13–12 overall, but there was a silver lining. The team was 4–2 against the larger schools in what would be called today the "power conferences." Outside of the Valley the Billikens beat Illinois, Ohio State, Kentucky, and Missouri, and lost to only Kansas State and Iowa. All eyes in St. Louis may have been on a construction site downtown on May 25, when Busch Stadium was to stage its groundbreaking.

For the record, no Big Ten team participated in the NIT. The teams of the Southwest Conference were absent, too.

On March 21, 1964 Duke lost the NCAA title to UCLA, a masterful team coached by a masterful man, John Wooden. This title was Wooden's first, with nine more to follow. The score of the game was 98–83, and people were talking of the lack of size and fantastic quickness of the Bruins. Wooden was busy setting the bar to a level impossible to duplicate. The Bruins were an impeccable 30–0.

Meanwhile, a fast-talking New Yorker was theorizing in Milwaukee about his team's chances in the future, should a "blue chip" recruit arrive. Al McGuire took over as Marquette coach on April 11, 1964, succeeding former Valley coach Eddie Hickey. In McGuire's first three seasons he went an unnoticed 2–1 versus Valley schools. Before long, the scene in Milwaukee resembled, in McGuire's own words, a "checkerboard."[6] He was plotting to recruit (more) black players from his native New York.

A very big kid was getting ready to move into the Valley, the University of Louisville. Located in the land of the mint julep and advanced equine studies, Louisville had veteran coach Bernard L. "Peck" Hickman at the helm, and he replaced home-and-home arrangements against Xavier, Eastern Kentucky, and Kentucky Wesleyan with games against the durable Valley. In the morning line, the Cardinals looked strong, since a large figure (pun intended) was getting ready to sign on at the school, Louisville's own Wes Unseld. Not so parenthetically, the *Sports Illustrated* piece on pre-season college basketball had informed the world with caution in the fall of 1963, "Louisville has its first Negro players."[7] (The U. of L. and the city held up their end of the deal. By the end of the 1966–1967 season the team would be averaging a Valley-leading 11,839 fans per game.)

The reason why competitive Louisville entered the Valley is found in the chart below: the team wanted stiffer competition, and found it. Perhaps the Big Ten, the Big Eight, and the Southwest Conference knew of that stiff competition, too?

TABLE 2 — MVC teams against the Big Ten, Big Eight, and Southwest Conferences

	1959–60	1960–61	1961–62	1962–63	1963–64	Total
Bradley	0–0	2–0	1–0	0–1	2–0	5–1
Cinn.	2–0	5–0	5–0	5–0	3–1	20–1
Drake	2–2	2–1	2–1	3–3	3–1	12–8
N. Texas	0–0	0–1	0–1	0–0	0–0	0–2
St. Louis	3–1	4–1	2–4	4–1	4–2	17–9
Tulsa	3–5	4–2	0–4	2–2	3–0	12–13
Wichita	0–0	6–1	4–1	4–1	4–2	18–5

The data overwhelms in **Table 2**. Who would have wanted to play Wichita (18–5 in the period)? Would a team have been crazy to play Cincinnati (20–1)? Only two teams, Tulsa and

North Texas, had losing records against the three conferences mentioned. Valley teams went a snappy 84–39 (.683) over the period, dazzling many of the teams against whom they played. The Woodens, the McGuires, and the Louisvilles were warned— think twice before taking on the Valley.

The Final Four, won by UCLA, was again played in centrally located Kansas City. In the years covered here the Bruins were a tidy 100–40 (.714), with even greater years to follow. All the teams got to Kansas City easily.

CHAPTER SEVEN

The Days Dwindle, 1964–1965

The spiraling down of the Valley's brilliance possibly began in the fall of 1964, when it dawned on people that one great coach, Ralph Miller at Wichita (220–133 over 13 seasons), was not returning. Who knew that four more coaches (Ed Jucker, Chuck Orsborn, Charles Johnson, and John Benington) were preparing to start their last season in the Valley? Joe Swank of Tulsa and Maurice John of Drake had to carry on, starting in 1965–1966.

Table 3, on the following page, showing the records of the seven teams during the five-year period, will get everyone's attention.

TABLE 3 – Overall records of MVC schools

	1959–60	1960–61	1961–62	1962–63	1963–64
Bradley	27–2	21–5	21–7	17–9	23–6
Cinn.	28–2	27–3	29–2	26–2	17–9
Drake	11–14	19–7	16–8	11–14	21–7
N. Texas	7–19	2–22	3–23	10–14	7–17
St. Louis	19–9	21–9	11–15	16–12	13–12
Tulsa	9–17	8–17	7–19	17–8	10–15
Wichita	14–12	18–8	18–9	19–8	23–6

The numbers were something. Bradley was an amazing 109–29, Cincinnati 127–18, St. Louis 80–57, Wichita 92–43, and Drake 78–50. Any coach would die for some of those numbers. Indeed, many coaching careers have died for want of those numbers.

How did the figures become so impressive? What was behind the Valley's success? The answers will come in a bit. But first things must be taken care of first.

The 1964–1965 season was rough on the two traditional heavyweights. Cincinnati lost twelve games overall, probably an omen about the beginning of the end of the world for the school's rooters. Cincinnati's Jucker had lost only 16 games *in the four seasons* prior to this one. Bradley had both high hopes and high prices for their home games ($40.00 for a chair-seat season ticket, $32.00 for a bleacher-seat ticket), but the team lost nine games amid 18 wins. At last, Bradley beat Cincinnati (by 16 and by 24!), but the Braves lost to Louisville twice. Even a championship win in the NIT the previous year was not strong enough to erase the hurt of nine losses experienced by the team on the Hilltop in Peoria.

Sixteen must have been a number of importance: the eligibility of Wichita star Dave Stallworth ran out after the sixteenth game of the year.[1] The team, obviously, was not the same once he stopped playing for the Shockers. They missed his 25 points per game.

Some may claim that absolute rock bottom was reached on January 27th, when the visiting Pumas of St. Joseph's College in Rensselaer, Indiana nipped the Bearcats of Cincinnati in the Queen City, 61–59, before 5,003 stunned fans. Cincinnati finished seventh in the Valley, an unthinkable state of affairs just a few months earlier.

More important things were happening outside the Valley on February 13th, to be sure. Vietcong attacked American barracks at Qui Nhon. The games no doubt looked very small.

Trophies were not so obvious after the 1964–1965 season, although Wichita did make the Final Four. The Shockers were ranked number one in the country on December 14. However, once in the NCAA tourney, the team went only 2–2, beating Southern Methodist University, 86–81, and Oklahoma State, 54–46, but losing by horrible scores to UCLA, 108–89, and to Princeton, 118–82. In the UCLA game, the Shockers were down 65–38 at the half, and in the game against Princeton, Bill Bradley lit up Wichita for 58 points for third place.[2] The Shockers should not have felt badly about their defeat to Bill Bradley and Princeton; the Tigers also mauled Providence, 109–69, with Bradley scoring 41 points! Dave Stallworth's eligibility was used up, of course.

Louisville had not made its powerful presence felt dramatically by this point. The team went 15–10 (8–6 MVC) in its first season in the Valley, but was getting stronger by the minute. Large Wes Unseld was poised to join the varsity team; he would give new meaning to the term "powerful rebounding."

In the NIT there was an eastern flavor to the games, although a significant name came from the west, Texas Western College (now the University of Texas at El Paso [UTEP]). (The school would go on to win the NCAA title in the spring of 1966.) Concerning the Valley in the NIT, St. Louis lost to Army by four, and Bradley lost to New York University by one in the first round. St. John's won the NIT; the championship game was the last one for veteran coach Joe Lapchick of the Redmen.

St. Louis, however, was doing well. It had a record of 5–1 versus Adolph Rupp and his Kentucky Wildcats since the 1959–1960 season. (One wonders if a basketball-rich school like Kentucky would tolerate today losing so frequently to a "small school" like St. Louis. Would not the series be unceremoniously ended in a flash by the larger school?)

The four coaches who left the Valley had impressive numbers. John Benington departed with an overall record of 118–71 (.624). His winning percentage was remarkably similar to that of last year's departure, Ralph Miller at Wichita. Benington would exit the Valley with a record of 5–2 against Kentucky. Chuck Orsborn left Bradley after a staggering overall record of 194–56 (.776) in nine years, and an incredible 127–38 (.770) from 1959–1960 until quitting time. Not to be outdone, Ed Jucker stepped down at Cincinnati with a log of 113–28 (.801) and two NCAA titles.

Charles Johnson at North Texas exited with a record of 29–95 (.234) against possibly the best talent in the nation.

Maybe the four coaches acutely felt that the rigors of coaching in the tough Valley could be avoided by going elsewhere. Benington was leaving St. Louis for Michigan State, joining the Big Ten, as Miller had done the previous year at Wichita (for Iowa). It seems the Big Ten was slow to play the Valley, but quick to hire its very good coaches. The two other coaches, Jucker and Orsborn, went on to other activities. With the advent of new coaches (and administrators), things were changing and becoming so crazy that Bradley would turn down an invitation to the NIT in the spring of 1966. The team was disappointed with its 20–6 record![3]

Veteran coaches remaining to battle things out in the Valley were Swank at Tulsa and John at Drake. John would later win some additional Valley Coach-of-the-Year awards, not to mention a scintillating Final Four appearance in 1969.[4]

Moving on, too, were Stallworth and his 1,936 points at Wichita, only 39 fewer than Bradley's Walker.

There was no sign of Iowa on Drake's schedule. That was odd since Frank "Bucky" O'Connor, a former Iowa coach, was a Drake graduate in 1938. He coached at Iowa from 1949–1950, and again from 1951–1952 until 1957–1958.

The season ended with UCLA winning the NCAA trophy over Michigan in Portland, Oregon. On the way there, the Bruins beat both Mormons (Brigham Young University) and Catholics (University of San Francisco). UCLA's Wooden was busy discussing leadership without self-indulgence, goals without quick gratification, and effort without limit.[5] The Bruins were a slick 28–2.

The country, however, was looking to expand beyond borders and boundaries in a different, and certainly more violent, fashion. Options and choices were winning the day; rules and regulations were not. With some irony, many waged war in American streets to protest the war in Southeast Asia.

College basketball recruiting was truly becoming a coast to coast affair, as (Ferdinand) Lewis Alcindor (now Kareem Abdul-Jabbar) announced in May that he was preparing to go from New York to Los Angeles to play at UCLA. He was 116–1 at a Catholic high school in the Bronx.[6] Having already captured the biggest trophy with no player near the ability (or the height) of Alcindor, the Bruins secured the best of the best. They would win three national titles and lose only two games in three years. The team would go 88–2 with Alcindor.

In the South, meanwhile, Coach Dean Smith of North Carolina would not be hearing of Charlie Scott until January of 1966. Scott would not be the first black recruited onto the UNC campus. That was William Cooper, who was a Tar Heel basketball recruit briefly.[7]

Times, and won-loss records, were changing.

CHAPTER EIGHT

Below the Surface

Is the story of the Valley's brilliance in men's basketball ended with the final horn at the end of the 1964–1965 season? Obviously not, if one wishes to ask some simple questions concerning certain issues in the sociology of the games.

Why did the Valley not play the Big Ten, the Big Eight or the Southwest Conference with some frequency if those schools were located in the same state(s) as the Valley schools? Or, better said, why did the schools in those well-known conferences not play the Valley regularly? After all, some of them (e.g., Kansas, Oklahoma State, Oklahoma, Iowa, and Missouri) were at one time or another in the Valley, and the Valley schools had not moved. Further, the "culture" in many cases was the same: the farms around Des Moines looked like the farms around Iowa City, and those farmers might have thought that a home-and-home series was a good idea. The football-crazy folks both in Texas and Oklahoma probably would have enjoyed a Valley school taking on a larger school just a few hours away by car. Could not Goliath have adjusted some priorities a bit and scheduled a tussle with David at least once in a while?

Why did Illinois play Bradley in 1936–1937, but not again until the 1973–1974 season? Why did Iowa not play Drake for so long? They met each other on February 3, 1936, but not again until December 11, 1965! Iowa State, it is true, was on Drake's schedule, but there was no sign of Iowa. The school was only 115 miles down the road. Columbia, Missouri was only 125 miles from St. Louis, but the schools did not play each other from March of 1949 until December of 1963. Why not? Also, was there a chance Valley newcomer Louisville would have been played by Kentucky? (Answer: no.)

First, did any institution find a problem in its travel plans during this period? Kentucky and South Carolina were able to make it to St. Louis (although both lost to the Billikens in the 1962–1963 season). North Dakota in the 1962–1963 season and Idaho State in 1963–1964 made it to Peoria. Washington State and Michigan arrived in Wichita in one piece (although both lost to the Shockers in the 1960–1961 season). Des Moines was not too far for Utah State in the 1959–1960 season, or for Dayton in the 1960–1961 term. Pacific and Duquesne were able to find Cincinnati (although both lost to the Bearcats in the 1958–1959 season).

School officials, after all, from Nebraska, Missouri, Kansas, and Iowa were able to get to Kansas City on February 16, 1907 for the second meeting in the history of the Conference. The session took place historically between the first flight of the Wright Brothers in 1903 and the release of the Model T in 1908, but everybody got there.

Further, once several of the big schools named above broke from the Valley in 1928, some teams practically had to go past the front door of Valley schools to complete their schedules as members of a differing conference. If Texas could go from its home in Austin to Norman, Oklahoma for a basketball game, could not Texas have gone to Tulsa for the same thing? Southwest Airlines flies the route today in only 105 minutes, and that is with a stop in Dallas. It is 495 miles by road, but only two hours, 32 minutes on a C-182 years ago. In football, both Oklahoma and Texas find "neutral" Dallas every year. Arkansas (in Fayetteville) has been finding Texas for a football game every year since 1894, but Tulsa had to find Fayetteville five times and neutral Little Rock twice for football games between 1959 and 1965; in those years Arkansas never came to Tulsa. Wichita and North Texas also visited Little Rock for football in 1964 and 1965 respectively, but neither school was given a return game by the Razorbacks. Little Rock to Wichita is 450 miles by road today, but only two hours and eight minutes on that same C-182 years ago. Oklahoma State dropped out of the Valley after the 1956–1957 season, and home-and-home games against in-state rival Tulsa started to diminish after the 1958–1959 season. The 90 miles between Urbana-Champaign and Peoria could not have been snowy all the time; Peorians covered more ground than that when they piled into busses in Peoria to go to the Chicago Stadium to see their Braves put a licking on Notre Dame.

Second, could money, or its lack, have been the reason? The crowds at Bradley were excellent at Robertson Field House. Ditto in Cincinnati, and the same with St. Louis, not to mention Wichita. Could not the Braves have paid Illinois to come in and play? (Imagine the ticket sales!) Huff Gym (cap. 6,900) at Illinois was a bit smaller than Robertson (8,000), but it would have been a nice payday for Illinois if the Illini had scheduled the Braves for a visit. The same goes for Missouri and St. Louis. (Imagine the soft drink sales!) The expense to go from Iowa City to Des Moines along old Route 6 could not have been an economic burden years ago; it is not expensive now along speedy Interstate 80.

Third, could the problem have been religion? Were people afraid that a Roman Catholic in the White House, John F. Kennedy, had the authority to command St. Louis, a university both Catholic and Jesuit, to schedule certain people and not others? Would St. Louis Catholics have put a curse on the visiting Missouri Tigers from Columbia during free throw attempts? The questions seem ridiculous. Lawrence H. Fuchs at Brandeis University in 1958 had warned about the danger of "fundamental and important value differences"[1] that distinguish one churchgoer from the next, but those fears seem to have been evaporating.

Fourth, how about the glories of good old-fashioned, face-to-face competition? Would not have Kansans from Goodland to Leavenworth have enjoyed Wichita and Kansas hooking it up? Would there not have been a good turnout (read: profit) for Oklahoma State to visit Tulsa? Those schools find each other today for a football game; was yesterday in basketball extremely different from today in football? (Does not Google interface well today, and commercially so, with Yahoo?) Would there not have been merit in going up in class a bit? If the Valley schools were thought to be worthy competitors, would not opposing players and coaches have wanted to play them?[2] Why not play excellent opposition to improve one's own team? (Imagine the T-shirt sales!)

Fifth, were there issues of presentation and identification? Valley players, coaches, and teams seemed to have shown themselves well to people, even though America was in figurative flames during this period. One reads of no incidents involving students doing horrible things at a Valley school, or a Valley school doing dreadful things to its students. Racial troubles took place at Central High School in Little Rock in 1957 and in 1963, but not at Edison High in Tulsa. Austin, Texas was the site of a shooting (at the University of Texas) in 1966, not Denton. The assassination of Dr. King took place in Memphis in 1968, not in Cincinnati in 1961 or in Des Moines in 1962.[3] In 1957 plans to improve the parking around the major league baseball park in Cincinnati inconvenienced many in the black community, but no harm came of it. In 1960 the city of Cincinnati had developed a plan for its Avondale-Corryville areas to improve life in the black community (and had ambitions everywhere to improve life in the white community); the situation was no-harm, no-foul. Both the city of St. Louis and St. Louis University were tranquil;[4] disappointment over the Pruitt-Igoe housing project (built in 1956) had not reached critical mass there yet. Citizens of Tulsa, "red" as well as white, were fine, and blacks there seemed in the early 1960's to have been "a credit to their race," as the hackneyed, race-based language would have it. There indeed were some awkward moments involving segregation and other social ills in Valley venues, but life moved along nevertheless.

Sixth, was there a small town/big city antagonism? Some may have thought that the six cities of the Valley (minus Denton in this frame) were denizens of drugs, divorce, and debauchery, but the evidence is insufficient. In truth, St. Louis saw its population decrease during the period, but things were not so bad. Cincinnati has had racial troubles recently, but not so much during the early 1960's. The biggest problem in small Denton might have been the lines in the cafeteria at Texas Woman's University in the fall of 1961. Did the presence of the Hiram Walker Distillery in Peoria frighten anyone from Champaign-Urbana or anywhere else? Was the Petroleum Building in Tulsa threatening to people from out of town who were not schooled in the oil business? Others came to Peoria and Tulsa for business and pleasure. Why not the big state schools for basketball games?

Seventh, were there difficulties with academic standards? Dick Harp of Kansas and Tex Winter of Kansas State seemed to have thought so. Harp spoke of wishing to have "the same scholastic requirements as the other teams," and Winter mentioned that Valley schools were accepting "marginal students."[5] However, Joe Stowell, a former head coach at Bradley (1965–1966 to 1976–1977), does not agree. He offers that academic requirements were not an issue when both Bradley and Kansas wanted the same prospect, 6 foot, 11 inch Walt Wesley, who eventually chose to play amid chants of "Rock Chalk, Jayhawk, KU!" at Kansas.[6]

Eighth, could there have been a rule change that altered everything? Such a change, after all, had doomed Texas Christian

University in football in the 1950's; the end of players going two ways was a disaster for the Horned Frogs. They were "a small school with a scrawny budget."[7] They couldn't afford to recruit the players, and went a bit over four decades between football bowl games, from the late 1950's until the late 1990's. (One may remember that South Carolina left the Atlantic Coast Conference in 1971 due to difficulties encountered at the intersection of academic requirements and football.) Was the 1.600 rule a problem? Did college basketball need to resurrect football's "Purity/Sanity Code" of 1948 in some form to regulate things?

The items mentioned above might have somehow contributed to a cumulatively negative status for Valley schools. To paraphrase Andrew Sullivan, the net worth of the Valley institutions may have been sufficient, but their stock quote was not as high as those of the larger universities that were their neighbors.[8] Why should an institution run the risk (the ignominy?) of possibly losing a game to a school with a smaller enrollment, if not a smaller significance in the mind of the state's movers and shakers? Issues of status may have been "in play."

Having at least partially exhausted some possible reasons above, what might be left?

The answer, or at least the beginning to part of the answer, is beneath one's nose, and longstanding.

CHAPTER NINE

And Below That...

What could have created the chasm isolating Valley schools from the larger ones, if the reasons above are discounted, or at least downplayed? What factors might have caused the lengthy separation (or divorce) of the schools? What events of the period were informing the minds and hearts of the people who were making decisions at the time?

The presence of black players on Valley rosters might have been a threat to the games, putting in jeopardy the existing structures that were holding up those games. (The term "Negro" had given way to "black" in the wake of the Black Power movement years ago.) The story preceded basketball's invention in 1891: black involvement in increasing numbers created circumstances that whites had to respond to, and could not avoid.[1] Issues of race were becoming not only easily configured in the mind, but also were visible and "real in their consequences."[2]

Beneath the stories involving men's basketball in the Valley (and who would play whom) there was an age-old yet continuing search for a narrative which could regulate if not clarify some black-white interaction. The narrative would have to be pleasant for those in the majority, firm for those not, and with little room for dialogue, especially for "them," if whites (or nonblacks) are defined as "us."

Various "scripts," after all, had been found in the pages of American history in abundance. Persons stood apart from citizens at the time of the Dred Scott decision in 1857. There were immigration acts of 1921 and 1924. (Today's multiculturalism may be another example.[3]) From Robert Penn Warren's mention of a "Great Alibi" in the South to his description of a "Treasury of Virtue" in the North, the doings of the nation have turned with frequency on finding a story that puts forward a pleasant agenda while attempting to control social behavior in the same motion. In today's language, the culture was looking for an "explanatory variable,"[4] or possibly a "scheme of interpretation."[5]

The world of college basketball five decades ago was perfect for those seeking such a narrative, since black basketball players were increasing in number slowly on rosters in the Valley and elsewhere, although admittedly not everywhere. Ohio State had three blacks on the team in the 1959–1960 season. In the 1961–1962 campaign two blacks played for St. Louis. Four played at that time for Cincinnati, and five were on Drake's roster. In 1962–1963, there were four black starters for NCAA champion Loyola of Chicago. In the 1963–1964 season, Ohio University, to pick a name, had two blacks on the team, although in the 1969–1970 season there was not one. In 1964, the first black was recruited to West Point by coach Bob Knight. In the 1965–1966 season the doors of racial affairs (read: segregation) were blown off, as Texas-El Paso won the NCAA trophy with five black starters against Kentucky, which started not one.[6] The increase in the numbers was not in equilibrium, but the figures were nevertheless changing, and a story to make everything "legitimate" was needed.

Jim Crow was rearing his ugly head as stories were being composed and as black players were being recruited, of course. Young men who could play basketball were often brought aboard to keep up with the athletic Joneses. As some schools added a black (or blacks), other schools had to make a choice: join 'em if it looks like you can't beat 'em, or risk losing and have to create a story to support the losing. People had to learn to add before being subtracted. Those in charge had to find a way to match "social structures and policies, on the one hand, and patterns of representation on the other."[7]

College basketball saw the need to add black participation into university life, as long as that participation "fit." Some schools probably did not wish to replicate life in Mississippi, a "closed society" one was told, although many did drag their feet when it came to adding black players. Something of a delicate balance had to be found.

While the recruiting terrain was mightily contested, it had an added dimension: a coach had to consider not only recruiting good basketball players, but also bringing aboard (some) good players who were black.[8] Charles H. Dow would have been proud: the value of landing a skilled black player far exceeded the price of that player, as long as the player produced. However, to paraphrase Dow in reverse, the price of acquiring an unsuccessful black player would have far surpassed the value of said player. Phrased differently still, a coach had *much* to lose if he recruited black players who were not successful on the court.

The case could be made, further, that if a black player and a white one were judged to be equal in skills by the coaching staff, most certainly the white one won the day. The black player had to be noticeably better. (Later, Marquette's McGuire often played his son, a white, over George Frazier, a black, between 1970–1971 and 1972–1973. The coach felt they both were accomplished on the court as well as well behaved off of it, but McGuire openly admitted he loved his own son more.)

The rest may be history, less theoretically. Black player after black player entered play in the Valley and elsewhere, though not everywhere, to be sure. A good number demonstrated adequate skills (or better), and thereby changed the landscape of basketball forever.

The record shows that some black players in the Valley took a place among the all-time scoring and rebounding leaders in some schools. No one scored more points at Bradley in the first three years of varsity eligibility than Chet Walker. (Later, Hersey Hawkins [1984–1985 until 1987–1988] scored 1,873 points, 102 fewer than Walker, in his first three years, and an astounding 3,008 in all four. Mitchell Anderson [1978–1979 until 1981–1982] scored an even 1,750 in his first three years, and a total of 2,341 overall.) Cleo Littleton at Wichita in the early 1950's was the first black player west of the Mississippi to score more than 2,000 career points. Wes Unseld did very well at Louisville. Ditto for Don Freeman of Madison, Indiana, who played not in the Valley, but at Illinois. Freeman registered 1,449 points in his career there.

Allowing blacks into the classroom was probably judged to be less of a risk than having them represent the alma mater on the basketball floor and make money. More than a few schools (outside the Valley, of course) did not break their necks to see that the players even arrived in class or made any progress toward a degree. (Full disclosure: many of those who were recruited were not supremely gifted academically in the first place, to be sure.) If the majority of the players had indeed flooded the classrooms and received straight A's, there would have been sociological mayhem: such a show of strength might have been too much for certain nonblacks to endure. Multiple dollars at the box office and a limited presence in the classroom were just fine.

More than a few coaches moved up the ladder due to the successes of black players, and some coaches probably wished they had recruited some (more) good black players. It was probably no secret that John Benington in 1965 (moving from St. Louis to Michigan State) and Ralph Miller in 1964 (from Wichita to Iowa) brought with them the conviction that they must recruit good black players to be competitive. Those two proved to be excellent recruiters of both black and white players.

Basketball dead ends, however, were encountered at some schools that were slow to recruit black players; Iowa and Iowa

State come easily to mind. Missouri, for its part, could have used some help, too; the school posted a losing record overall in the years studied here. Footballer Bill Burrell of Illinois once summarized the situation, remarking that from 1956 until 1960 a black player at Illinois was "seldom allowed to start."[9] As recently as the 1973–1974 season there was not one black player on the Illinois basketball roster, and the team went 5–18 that year. (Lou Henson was on the way to Illinois from New Mexico State, where he had very successfully recruited black players.)

Indeed, some very good black players were coming and going in asymmetrical ways. While there may not have been much of a pipeline between Illinois and the Chicago public schools in the 1960's, Cazzie (Lee) Russell from Carver High in Chicago was indeed a "big name" who chose to go elsewhere—to Michigan. He led the Wolverines to the Final Four twice, in the spring of 1964 as a sophomore and in the spring of 1965 as a junior. (Bradley tried hard to get him!) Adolph Rupp at Kentucky did not have a black in his starting five when Marquette (with four) beat them in March of 1969; Tom Payne, a black, was still two months away from being a Wildcat. Tom Hawkins was the only black player at Notre Dame in the 1958–1959 season; the 1960–1961 team had not one. Louisville entered the Valley in 1965, won the men's basketball crown in 1967 (with Unseld and Alfred "Butch" Beard!), but curiously had no blacks on the freshman team in the 1966–1967 season. Several black players from New York City (e.g., George Thompson, Dean Meminger, *ut supra*) went to Milwaukee to play at Marquette, bypassing any number of schools in the process. Southern Illinois University in Carbondale successfully recruited several blacks (e.g., Walt Frazier, Joe Meriwether) from the south.[10] Some may remember that Jerry Sloan, a white, went out of state to Evansville, a short drive to the east of his home in McLeansboro, Illinois, but few may recall that he was joined in Evansville by a black young man, Larry Humes, Indiana's Mr. Basketball in 1962.

Personal and collective mixing may have been more difficult as one went in a southerly direction in the Valley, of course. The gestures shown to blacks by people in Peoria and Des Moines were maybe more gentle than the ones demonstrated by people (with a red neck?) below the 40th parallel. Such was "the Southern way of life," after all. Oscar Robertson once found a black cat in the locker room in Denton in January of 1959. Bradley and North Texas cleared their benches one night in Denton when some of the black Braves were playing well, maybe too well, against some of the white Eagles. Living among people who whispered the name of Jim Crow in the north was maybe a bit softer than seeing a sign "Colored Only" in the south, and doing something about it. The "Cotton Curtain" was rather firm.

The efforts to integrate (or desegregate or segregate) were chaotic, at random, and haphazard across America over the years. In 1960, about the time Oscar Robertson was scoring points at will on the basketball court (and acting like a gentleman off of it), three black young men were sitting at a whites-only lunch counter in Greensboro, North Carolina, and were getting a few stares, to say the least. Also in 1960, black golfer Charlie Sifford got a Tour card for the first time (when he was 38 years old, past his prime). In 1961 baseball's Negro Leagues had almost disappeared, but "freedom rides" certainly had not; President Kennedy had received a note from CORE Director James Farmer, who said that such rides needed federal protection. (Such protection would appear for all to see on that "vast wasteland," television.) In 1962 Judge John Minor Wisdom wrote that interracial boxing matches in Louisiana should in no way be segregated. In 1963 there were important events everywhere: George Wallace spoke clearly of the "benefits" of segregation, and a church in Birmingham was bombed,[11] but black faces displayed a look of optimism nevertheless at the March in Washington and elsewhere.[12] Further, James Baldwin's *The Fire Next Time* moved black literary and intellectual life into the American academy. In 1964, when the term "civil rights" was becoming a household phrase, both predominantly black Crispus Attucks High School in Carbondale, Illinois and predominantly black St. Elizabeth High School in Chicago were closing.[13] (Wouldn't one think the two schools would have been kept open, so that blacks would be kept separate and not be "a problem" to those who were not black?)

Issues of race were becoming more visible in the nation, not less. In 1965 President Johnson had his Texas-size hands full: in late January he was given a memo about "disastrous defeat" in Vietnam, and in early June he had to shift his focus to "affirmative action" at a talk at Howard University in Washington, mentioning "inherited, gateless poverty."[14] In 1969 the Texas Longhorns were the last all-white team to win the mythical national title in football.

Boundaries and borders were shifting, if not being shattered, in many social groupings. Elvis Presley swiveled, sang, and "sounded black," although he was a white Negro, to borrow from

Norman Mailer's 1957 essay. Some whites went to Mississippi to stand next to blacks and do some protesting. A young man with a changed name (Bob Dylan, from Zimmerman) arrived in New York City in 1961 to sing a "protest song" or two. In that same year comedian Lenny Bruce, frequently in trouble with the law, played Carnegie Hall and made his legal difficulties part of his act. Catholic leaders at their Second Vatican Council (1962–1965) in Rome were so bold as to urge women "to assume their full proper role in accordance with their own nature."[15] Homosexual people were starting to want a more vocal involvement in public life as well. At decade's end, Pete Maravich of Louisiana State was passing and shooting the basketball from every direction, thereby "playing black," although he was white. The days of "well-rounded truths," in the words of Parmenides, these were not.

The social shifting was not totally lost on black entertainers. The sway of the Four Tops' "Baby, I Need Your Lovin'" in 1964 was to give way to the bombast of the Temptations' hard-charging "Ball of Confusion (That's What the World is Today)" in 1970. Music critics noticed with glee that the sounds of Motown were absorbed nicely into the mainstream culture, unlike jazz and other genres at an earlier time. Mellow, for its part, would make a pleasant return with the Stylistics in the early 1970's.[16] To borrow from psychologist Rollo May, there were "profound convulsions of a transitional period."

The research of Charles H. Martin helps to sharpen the focus on what was happening on the basketball court and on the football field as far back as the 1930's, and as recently as the 1960's. He notes that a gentlemen's agreement was in place, whereby coaches and administrators agreed to think twice about playing a black player of their own when a school from the South did not have a black player, or did not want to play against such a player.[17] Fair was fair, after all, especially if that fairness had been defined as both teams having to exclude or limit nonwhite players. Further, fair would not have been fair if any manner of restrictions had been put on the white players. Fair was not fair if one school fielded a black player who could athletically dominate some or all of those around him. "Games" were played behind the real games. Common sense may have said that several good players were likely not included, since they were of a differing skin color from those who were included.[18] Many fans probably saw only that "their team" won or lost.

Martin includes the Valley in his research, commenting that the Valley had agreed in December of 1947 to stop racial discrimination by September of 1950.[19] Agreeing was one thing, however, and making it happen was another. One person's *de jure* integration may have been another person's *de facto* segregation. The Valley schools may have been doing their best in accepting black players, anticipating the day when college basketball (in Division I, at least) would be a showcase of black talent.

When asked face to face about an unwritten (and unspoken?) agreement to regulate black participation, certain people involved in Valley games years ago were not clear on why the big schools did not schedule the Valley teams. Clarence "Sonny" Means, an assistant coach at St. Louis University under John Benington in the early 1960's, says that he knew of no such agreement in force years ago. Means also mentioned that he does not have an easy answer about why the big (and bigger) schools did not play the Valley, except maybe that the rival schools had a hunch they would get beat.[20] Bradley's Stowell says he was not aware of anything racial happening in the background, although he smiled broadly when asked if he thought teams outside the Valley believed that they would get beat when playing the Valley.[21] Referee Richard Weiler, who came into the Big Ten in 1964 and also worked Valley games, said that the larger schools "were afraid of the L," referring to possible losses incurred when taking on the Valley.[22]

Means, Stowell, and Weiler chose not to reference the football game of Valley members Drake and Oklahoma State on October 20, 1951, when Drake football star Johnny Bright, a black, was intentionally injured, causing Drake to leave the Valley for a while.[23] Officials in the Valley looked the other way at the incident. The group's psychosocial poise was apparently not disturbed. (In the vernacular of today, what was black about it? Nothing.)

What was going on? A great deal, including the social ramifications of adding, little by little, young black men to Valley rosters and to rosters of (certain) other schools. Play was different, to be sure, and improved, not to mention loaded with significant social meanings throughout.[24]

CHAPTER TEN

Some Things Unfold

Although racial issues were not generated solely by the parties named above in the Valley and elsewhere, blacks and whites nevertheless intersected there with significant consequences.[1] The intersection took place haphazardly both across the entire land and in the Valley, setting into motion the need to ask a few questions many years after the fact about how to interpret some of the behaviors of those passing through that intersection. Were there mental and social "emotions, slants, and confusions"?[2] What forms of black and white interaction were problematic? What issues of interaction possibly caused some misunderstandings, and for that matter could be learned from today?

The situation may turn on a few "as-structures,"[3] as well as some seeing and being seen, as those actions are performed through a prism of race. Examining what people saw and how people "see (others) as" may enlighten the relations remembered years ago in the Valley. The eye may have been winning the battle with the ear in those days.[4]

A first step must be to say that white people did not see themselves as belonging to any particular racial group (with an appreciative nod to those who have explained that race is a difficult term on a good day). Although whites saw others (read: nonwhites) to be connected "racially" to those with a matching skin color, whites did not see themselves to be connected to fellow whites who, in the minds of whites again, have little or no color about them. One author comments that racial trouble is easily reproduced thereby, "without active participation by individual whites, and hidden from their view."[5] (John Fiske would use the word "exnomination.") Whites lived as if color (including white) were not in the field of play at all. Another person writes:

> Whites define our position on the continuum of
> racism by the degree of our commitment to color-
> blindness; the more certain of an individual's
> abilities or achievements, the more certain we are
> that we have overcome racism as we conceive
> of it. This way of thinking about race is a matter
> of principle as well as a product of historical
> experience. It reflects the traditional liberal view
> that the autonomous individual, whose existence
> is analytically prior to that of society, ought
> never be credited with, nor blamed for, personal
> characteristics not under her own control, such as

gender or race, or group membership or social
status that is a consequence of birth rather than
individual choice or accomplishment.[6]

The visual limitations on the part of whites were not due to
any white person living in darkness, nor to the physical property
of light. There was no physiological limitation of the eye, either.
The case turns on the conditions surrounding the ability to see in
ways more complicated than looking at the forms and objects in
front of a person's very eyes. Limited vision probably prevented
whites from asking, "Why can't we (whites) be more like them
(blacks)?" There always was, however, "Why can't they (blacks)
be more like us (whites)?"

Perhaps the only thing that certain (white) eyes saw were
in-the-flesh, interactional "broken windows,"[7] meaning that
certain items were noticed, like an occasional nonwhite person
doing a menial job in a particular venue, or some other nonwhites, possibly small in number, performing on a "stage" a few
feet away. (White is, after all, "the addition of all hues" to some
people,[8] although to others it is "the absence of color."[9]) In just
one sentence, a white person might have seen "blackness but only
through (superior) whiteness."[10]

A second critical turn takes place when whites outwardly
claim that although they saw and see blacks "clearly," they also
say that they selectively and mysteriously *do not* and *did not* see
them. White observers frequently declare that they see all others
in only one way—the one that references and attempts to
establish the presence of a level social playing field. (Inwardly,

of course, the story differs; the seeing is more difficult, and the field is seldom level. How could color not be seen if society's structures are built firmly on it? The field is decidedly not level.)

Of course, there are benefits for selected people if there is to things a certain "transparency."[11] The folly of the statement about one-way vision is revealed when one asks how a white person might see Oprah Winfrey or Michael Jordan. Must they not be seen as black at once? Or as black and successful? Or as successful, first, and black, second? Or, somehow, as neither one? For this matter, cannot Oprah or Michael Jordan be seen as wealthy?[12] (How is singer Michael Jackson seen by blacks? How by whites? As black or beige, or in a style that has nothing to do with color? As *totaliter aliter*? In this matter is it not essential to admit that it is more convenient for the majority to say what a white person is not, than to define what one is?) Could whites in Cincinnati not see that Oscar Robertson was black? Of course they could see that he was black, but the narrative *du jour* was to bifurcate what Robertson and others did on the court from what he (and they) did off of it. The argument about color-blindness possibly references the wordings of the mid-1960's when blacks and white marched together, claiming that they saw no color among them.[13] (Yes, times have changed, or maybe they never have changed at all.)

The truncated vision on the part of whites (in the majority) keeps neighbors (in the minority) at a manageable distance, while buying time for those in the majority to think of their next response in the narrative.[14] Achromatic people with limited eyesight were positioned not only to fortify themselves at least externally before nonwhites, but also never to have to question why their vision was the way it was. Vision is "intrinsically active,"[15] and "seeing is power."[16] Some never had to question what was going on. Why, therefore, labor to fix something that is not only perceived to be unbroken, but is indeed in itself a thing of power? Meanwhile, others who were not white became outsiders at best, occupying a place of secondary importance.[17]

Whites with impaired vision saw little reason to acknowledge or remedy problems experienced by nonwhites, therefore, since participation by nonwhites in the public forum and on Valley basketball courts was purposefully limited by time and space. On the court, play was configured carefully by time and space. The refusal of whites to reach out beyond the courts and games was encased in the invisible: people of color were no longer on the main stage, and they therefore were not seen very much. There can be, in the wording of Patricia J. Williams, a "rationalized irrationality" to things.[18] The confines of time and space allow lines to be drawn and enforced in order for the general population to live and prosper; time and space were not thereby configured for the minority to share issues important to them. Whites, instead, were busy making efforts to receive what may be called both "self-confirmatory feedback,"[19] and the concomitant right to choose others with whom to interact. Some people did not, to use the words of Josef Albers, "see in situations," and they therefore saw no reason to reach out to others not like themselves.

At sidebar, such a privileged stance brings with it some interesting unintended consequences: today whites occasionally say that they even feel deprived (somehow) as a group, asking why there is no holiday for a person such as Robert F. Kennedy, when there is such a day for Dr. King. (Both were assassinated in the same year [1968], only a matter of weeks apart.) The effects of the "blindness" still come to the surface in any number of places.[20] In the words of Malcolm Gladwell, there was no "thin-slicing" necessary: the street (or the look?) went only one way.[21]

In turn, blacks saw clearly that they indeed did need whites to get somewhere in life. Whites were "ascendant" in Valley affairs and elsewhere years ago, and blacks probably saw that ascension clearly, for there were no black head coaches or black athletic directors for a person to see, never mind to relate to or work with. Black assistant coaches were unheard of at the time, as were black head coaches and black athletic directors.[22] There were no black referees, either. Some would say breezily, "Black is the subtraction of all hues."[23] Blacks were "accommo-dating selves," in the words of James Mark Baldwin, needing to adjust their narratives accordingly. Although the Valley had wished to drive out discriminatory practices by 1950, as mentioned earlier, not that much had changed either in the Valley or in the general population.[24]

In essence, the black players years ago were "known to be seen" by the general (read: white) population. Who could not recognize Oscar Robertson both off the court and on? Who did not imagine himself gliding gracefully to the basket like Chet Walker? Who would not recite in the same motion Justice John Marshall Harlan's claim about the Constitution and the American people being color-blind?

"Known to be seen" is established by two facts. First, all the Valley schools enrolled a few black students among many nonblack ones, and second, the roles played by the black players were clearly defined, if not obvious. The few were where they were to play basketball in a public and purposeful way. Sociologist Harry Edwards, who is black, has said quite bluntly, "Blacks are brought in to perform."[25] To this day, Bradley, a private school, has a few black students, but not very many. The same description might apply, *mutatis mutandis*, to Drake and Wichita. A 6 foot, 9 inch black young man walking across either campus today brings two words to mind on the part of many whites, at least: basketball player. "Known to be seen" (in the passive voice for grammarians as well as for social scientists) was part and parcel of the performances of players like McCoy McLemore at Drake, Levern Tart at Bradley, and Kelly Pete at Wichita (all black). Fans could fasten a name to a face, but probably could not share a significant personal or social detail about a black player. Did many people care that George Unseld, brother of Wes of the University of Louisville, would leave both the city of Louisville and the state of Kentucky for Lawrence, Kansas not only to play basketball, but also to become involved in sit-ins in Lawrence? There is little data to suggest that anyone cared.

Off the court, however, the players were seldom "seen (in order) to be known." Who wanted to converse with Dave Stallworth about issues important to black people? Why talk to Tony Yates of Cincinnati about his upbringing? Were the opinions of Donnell Reid of St. Louis ever asked? (Does the occasion not recall Ralph Ellison's work on invisibility?) Acquaintances were not pursued and topics of possible mutual interest beyond basketball were for the most part not mentioned after the game(s). Chet Walker writes that he "was never invited to anything,"[26] and he offers that people "wanted to be seen with me in certain places, in controlled situations."[27] The players were seen to be enjoyed by the general population, and indeed were so, although they were not necessarily heard from, or engaged, away from the court.

Importantly, the "double consciousness" of blacks mentioned by W. E. B. Du Bois in 1903 went only one way, that is black viewing white, and there has been no "guide book" for those who are white but must "view black." Du Bois writes that the black man inhabits "a world which yields him no true self-consciousness, but only lets him *see* [italics mine] himself through the revelation of the other world. It is a peculiar sensation, this double consciousness, this sense of always *looking at* [italics mine] one's self through the eyes of others, of measuring one's soul by other tape of the world that *looks on* [italics mine] in amused contempt or pity."[28] How right he had it.

In the Valley the black athlete saw very little, except a sea of white faces at the games, a scoreboard revealing some numbers, and statistics in a box score. (What was a Rebel flag or two in the stands in St. Louis?) Charles Horton Cooley and his "looking glass" theory would have contributed, "The self is a result of the social process whereby we learn to see ourselves as others see us."[29] Blacks had to tailor their behavior according to the gaze of whites, while whites seldom had to adjust to the looks of others, and therefore probably saw very little to fear.

Whites first and foremost did not have to fear being not white, and they did not have to fear having to jump through hoops (one must pardon the expression) put in place by people who were not white.[30] The last player off the bench at Tulsa was playing with house money, enjoying a place on the team, but having to work hard during the practices. Not producing during games may not have been a big worry, however.

Never mind that white people probably did not see non-whites as people who were owed much of anything; they were, in a word, "nonpersons."[31] The official articulation of the relation was that the players, both black and white, were student-athletes and had a "scholarship," although the word in truth seems to have been a stretch in some cases. The humorous aside that gets a laugh is that one must strain mightily at times to find a graduate, any graduate, who can verify that a certain student-athlete (black or white) sat in the same classroom with other students at any time during the student-athlete's years of eligibility.[32]

It was certainly much easier for whites to retire the number of an excellent player (e.g., the number 12 of Oscar Robertson at Cincinnati) than to pursue black issues in the concrete. Retiring a jersey is seen to be magnanimous, and the recipients are well advised to look appreciative. The memorializing of the numbers establishes a zone of psychic and behavioral comfort between the fans and the players. A person committed to the memory can be frozen in time, and therefore is not a threat. Further, a plaque gives information that is not necessarily internalized with a great deal of commitment or care. A result is sociological "cheap talk" among the fans, generating the conditions for pleasant conversation between various individuals and groups while binding no one to much of anything.[33]

The situation, in sum, may have resembled a Doppler effect of the eye, not the ear: both whites and blacks had to shift their narratives in a flash given the presence of the "unfamiliar" other, with whites clearly holding command of most social structures and their outcomes.

CHAPTER ELEVEN

On a Philosophical Note

Perhaps much of the story for both blacks and whites turns with frequency on the social and philosophic world of "as if," a tiny conjunction that puts its users in a world of "comparative apperception," to use the words of its foremost proponent.[1] The words put those who utter them in a world of fiction, since "a whole sentence lies implied."[2] Both groups seemed to have been living there years ago.

Black players, few that there were in the Valley of yesteryear, were treated by whites *as if* they were kings and heroes, as long as they performed well. Black players were tasked to provide a favorable final score for the fans and "their" school, and often did. Cincinnati was a brilliant 79–9 with Oscar Robertson in the lineup![3] Chet Walker was an excellent 69–14 at Bradley. On the other side, John Savage was a woeful 20–54 at North Texas; no ill will came his way because the fans of the Eagles knew he was doing his level best on three poor teams in a very tough conference. He scored 1,423 points in his three-year career, 19.2 points per game. It may have been that Savage was treated *as if* he had been a "smaller version" of Walker or Robertson. (Perhaps Tulsa was clearly living in a world of *as if*, since there was not a black player on the team during this period. The Hurricane played *as if* the team could be successful without black players, or maybe *as if* there had not been a black young person who could play college basketball at the time.)

Off the court, black players were somewhat invisible, although frequently not for their size or their color. Once off the "stage" at Bradley (the court, that is, a veritable 28 inches above the floor years ago) and once away from the Roundhouse at Wichita, a low profile was a must. Such a profile included life lived predominantly in the present moment; such is always the style of children, or at least the style of young men cast as (obedient!) children. This world of make-believe becomes obvious when one recalls the old line, "How did a 6 feet, 9 inch black young man become difficult to see on a campus that was less than five percent black?" The players had to conduct themselves *as if* they were "student-athletes" like other people, and *as if* they could easily blend in. Of course, they could not easily blend in, and were subject (or "object") to a differing and changing set of social rules compared to their white "brothers."

Blacks framed individual gestures and commentary with care certainly. Kelly Pete of Wichita performed *ad libitum* ("according to his wishes") within the confines of the game, and his wordings were doubtless formulaic after the game: he was happy to do his part, the game was exciting, and the crowd was really behind the (home) team. Larry Prins, a white player from Drake, certainly lived in a different world, and could converse more daringly about things: it was a great win for the team, the coach was at the top of his game, etc. Pete would defeat Prins for oral predictability hands down. Oscar Robertson once scored 62 points against North Texas in 1960 and responded succinctly in an interview, "Had fun tonite."[4] In Mead's terms, he was putting the attitudes of other persons into his own conduct, and in Morris Rosenberg's he was probably weighing carefully his "reflected appraisals" of himself. A wider or deeper perspective was not allowed.

The most precious things in the world were denied to the black players, that is the sharing of personal and collective stories that framed their very existence. One cannot find anywhere near St. Louis, either at the university and or in the city, Donnell Reid's accounts of growing up. Ditto for Alfred Nickleberry of North Texas. The obvious and the personal became inexpressible. Whites, meanwhile, shared stories with abandon about the night their favorite black player (and team) lit up the opposition and provided victory for the alma mater. Not mentioned was the ownership of a white upbringing that did not include interaction with as few as two black persons in the process.

Why the distancing? What is implied here? Maybe *as if* strikes again.

White perception and evaluation held sway.[5] White fans and administrators, many that there were, were treated by black players *as if* they (whites) were informed spectators and sole proprietors of and through all, and whites acted in turn *as if* the blacks on the court were at least in the moment acceptable in all areas associated with the game(s). Season ticket holders were predominantly white, many of the fans were white, and great pride in the team's success (often powered by blacks) was shown by whites. Maybe they (whites) were saying things to themselves that altered what they were seeing, or thought that they were seeing.[6] Having little background about the details surrounding black lives, the whites had to furnish their own story lines about racial differences and their workings. The letter of white law trumped the spirit of the black.

To paraphrase Gerald Early, the true threat that blacks posed for the larger population was not dissimilarity or its visible effects, but similarity, with its own effects. When people raise a problem over the behavior of others (especially the behavior of those with a differing skin color), they are more often than not largely motivated by envy rather than by disgust.[7] How many white players and fans would have wanted to play like Robertson, Walker, and Stallworth? Probably a ton of them, yet officially and silently the narrative stipulated that black players and the team's (white) followers were to be segregated at nearly every turn, keeping potential hostilities to a minimum. Whites were entrusted with the most important task of all in this relation, the maintenance of the balance of power, come what may. To recall James P. Carse for a moment, blacks were finite players playing within boundaries, while whites were infinite players playing with boundaries.

Both blacks and whites existed in a separate epistemic and interpersonal limbo. Vaihinger describes the "as if" to be "*eine Erdictung oder wenigstens etwas der Erdichtung sehr Verwandtes*" ("an invention or at least something very similar to an invention" [translation mine][8]). What could be more fictitious than white fans trying to relate to what young black men were doing both with great skill on the court and in society's margins off of it? What could be more fictitious than black young men trying to picture a white-collar, $75,000-a-year job after graduation?

This story of the Valley may end where most investigations start—in a type of relational "thin air" that may recall philosopher George Berkeley, who theorized that some things are seldom im-mediately [*sic*] seen or with great precision judged. So it may have been with issues of vision and presentation both in the Valley and in the general population many years ago: the fictional nature of the "as if" relation obscured the vision of both blacks viewing whites and whites viewing blacks.

While black players were not the clear property of whites, which would have suggested an earlier context larger than basketball in the Valley, the relation could be described as "com-modified."[9] Time spent on the court by black players was translatable into a substantial amount of money for those not black, and into some pretty nice times by those not white. Although bargaining and exchange were not so obvious, the risk of taking black players onto the roster was converted into a dollar figure to be gained by a team playing its regular season games, to say nothing of a team being invited to post-season play for even greater financial gain. The economic side was possibly as veiled as the gentlemen's agreement(s). It may have been a short walk from having impaired vision to making poorly conceived decisions about the lives of others to believing that one has a sense of entitlement that others do not have.

Conclusion

On the front stage, the seven-team Missouri Valley Conference enjoyed outstanding success in men's basketball, winning national championships and gaining much national attention in the process. Cincinnati and Bradley were able to take on, and convincingly defeat, anyone; Drake, St. Louis, and Wichita State were also formidable, probably capable of beating a majority of the nation's teams a majority of the time. Tulsa had to hang on for dear life, and poor North Texas was the doormat.

In the back, the recruiting of black players to Valley campuses generated some interesting social patterns, since a few large universities, in many cases geographically close to Valley schools, chose at the same time not to recruit black players, or at least did not get them. The so-called public universities existed in their own "morphology," so to say. Not having black players meant that the large schools would hesitate to schedule games against Valley teams, or would avoid them entirely. One can only wonder what the games would have looked like, with the large, at times nearly lily-white schools opposing the smaller schools with some stellar black players.

A "gentlemen's agreement" was installed silently in order to regulate and safeguard the social and interactive "face" of the games. How else to cope with the situation, given that the civil rights movement, in at least Gerald Early's description, was still only about two decades old? (On each December 1st in Valley venues there was no public mention of the anniversary of the refusal of Rosa Parks to move on a Birmingham bus, or the $14.00 fine levied against her. Such a gesture was unheard of at the time.) The agreement, unwritten of course, stipulated that the number of black players on a given team could "roughly" equal in number, but not surpass, that of an opposing team. A level playing field could be guaranteed thereby. Administrators and fans, in the majority naturally, were not comfortable socially or competitively with the prospect of losing to teams that had recruited players willy-nilly "from the minority." Losing a harmless basketball game was never really and truly thought to be harmless, of course.

Cases of impaired vision, or in some people a veritable blindness, may have been a problem for both the majority and the minority in this intersection. White administrators and coaches saw black players to be "representing" their school on the court, and those players were to be in narrow and quiet configurations off of it. Who cared what the players did between the games, provided that they produced during those games? In turn, black players possibly saw only what they were allowed to see: final scores, their own statistics, and enthusiastic fans. Issues of larger import to black people (e.g., housing, jobs, and education) were not seen by whites, never mind jointly addressed by both blacks and whites. How could "black issues" arrive at the desks of whites, given this limited vision? Were not blacks too busy just trying to get by? How could whites interface with blacks, given that whites were busy preserving structures of control and power? Was this not a "world of strangers," to use Lyn Lofland's 1973 term?

Not least, selective attention and shifting took place amid social conditions that were becoming at the time chaotic in the general population, if not contradictory, for both blacks and whites. In some cases the desegregation of one institution took place down the block from the segregation of another, all for seemingly noble and sound reasons, like keeping the peace (again), "helping" those in the minority, and paying the bills. Blackness was to be celebrated, although at times it encountered a posted "right to refuse service." Whiteness was dominant, and in truth more than a few whites probably never saw a problem in that dominance.

The unruly social climate of the period may have been at the core idealistic, both in a common-sense and philosophic way, for both sides. A better day for both blacks and whites was promised, although the measures to guarantee the arrival of that day seemed to have been unclear. Possibly similar to the views of Berkeley two centuries earlier, it might have been that certain items were perceived but not well understood, suspected flimsily but judged with firmness nevertheless. Did people of an "opposing" skin color truly exist if they were not perceived clearly and with some depth? Did whites see the shape of the tree, but not its substance? Color and little else? Physicist Lawrence M. Krauss says with frequency that what we see is far from all that there is.

Maybe blacks and whites saw themselves *as if* each group had much to lose, and little to share, should they interact. Neither saw reasons to change behavior to facilitate interaction: whites may have feared change, while blacks may have been frozen in time and space, not allowed to change if the world (or the conference title) depended on it. No political revolution from above and no social transformation from below took place. While the country was rocking (and roiling) on the outside, perhaps a confining status quo prevailed for both groups on the inside.

The fictitious world of "as if" has been exposed a bit over the years, since some successful mingling on the court and off has changed things, of course. The additional numbers of blacks created a greater access to a college education, a larger opportunity for blacks to use their voice in the community, and a better chance for the schools to make even more money, to say nothing of the wider perspective gained by whites intersecting with blacks. Although some would make the case that a collegiate athletic contest exists "as if it's always being performed for a white audience,"[1] it is true nevertheless that college basketball has flourished since the years covered in this volume, possibly because some problems of race have been overcome a bit in the process.

While Pete Hamill has said that news involves verbs, maybe it can be claimed that a game involving Valley teams displayed some other elements of grammar as well. In the ergative mood, the "subjects," a few black players, were "marked" in a contrasting way when compared to the "objects," many white players. Black players were therefore constricted, while white ones behaved more freely than blacks. Both, in effect, ended up to be objects to one another, being perceived in "raw" and functional ways. Neither understood the other very much.

Perhaps Chet Walker of Bradley put it best when he spoke of an existence "between anonymity and fame."[2] Black players had to perform (well!) in a very measured environment, and at the same time had to understand the import of the bright lights that were following them on the court, but certainly not off of it.

Meanwhile, issues of race today are again submerged of course in the affairs of college basketball, although the numbers of black players have increased significantly, and media guides reveal mostly numbers of a differing kind. They show Bradley going 2–12 all-time against Illinois as of June 2005, and John Benington of St. Louis coaching against the University of Missouri only twice.[3] The figures do not show that Illinois refused to schedule Bradley for more than 35 years; imagine what the Braves would have done to the Illini from the late 1950's into the mid-1960's. Further, no documents are found today which broadcast that Missouri turned down games against Benington and his Billikens. Ditto for the two large public universities in Kansas against mighty Wichita State. And the media guides do not show black-white interaction. (The guides, to be fair, do not exist for that reason.)

On the court there is ample opportunity to study today's Valley, a total of ten teams in six states, with only three members from the configuration mentioned here. The conference is holding its own, but it is still not a large showcase like the Big Ten or the Big East.[4] (The Valley does not need to be, or try to be.) The numbers did show, however, that on January 31, 2006 the Valley was fifth in the conference Ratings Percentage Index.[5] Both Wichita State and Bradley made it to the Sweet 16 that year. A return to even the Elite Eight on the national stage may be a few years off, to be sure.

Perhaps all the issues mentioned here would go well in a Tulsa church on a Sunday morning. The minister could preach about the words of St. Paul in Second Corinthians 4:17–18, who writes, "… we look not to the things that are seen but to the things that are unseen; for the things that are seen are transient, but the things that are unseen are eternal." Skin color was indeed seen, and possibly little else, years ago. The need to look and live beyond color and its social meanings was not exactly nurtured or cultivated, but should be today.

Maybe all should see race for what it is—a bankrupt construct on which American life has been built for far too long.

The Missouri River has been labeled "a highway into the west,"[6] and Lewis and Clark were to study the "soil and face of the country." Perhaps this work has provided an inroad into seeing a different face to college basketball several years ago.

Endnotes

Introduction

1. John W. Heisman remarked about the possibility of awarding a trophy in 1935, "Is it not meant to exemplify the grandeur of a thousand men?"

2. Orlando Patterson, "A Poverty of the Mind," *New York Times*, March 26, 2006, sec. 8, p. 13.

Chapter One: Of Farms and Factory

1. It is not easy to remember which schools comprised the Valley in the beginning days, in part because several institutions were coming, going, coming, and going. In 1907 Missouri, Iowa, Nebraska, Kansas, and Washington University were indeed playing football against one another, but one school played one conference game, three played two, and one played three. In 1908 Iowa went 0–4 in the Valley, but 0–1 in the Big Ten Conference! In 1909 schools played either two, three, four, or five games against one another! By 1911 Iowa was gone, although Iowa State was staying. To confuse matters, some sources say that the Valley and the Big Eight Conference share "a similar history," but do not bother to explain the who, the what, or the why of the situation.

2. Some names have changed. North Texas State College became North Texas State University in 1961. Teams there are labeled Mean Green today. Wichita became Wichita State in 1964. Oklahoma A&M became Oklahoma State on July 1, 1957; the school will be called Oklahoma State hereafter.

3. Carl Abbott, "College Athletic Conferences and American Regions," *Journal of American Studies*, vol. 24, no. 2 (August 1990), p. 217. The word "conference" means a "bringing together," and the seven schools under study here were able to be brought together from the fall of 1960 until the spring of 1964, when powerful Louisville was preparing to come in. The first of the seven to leave after the 1959–1960 season was Cincinnati in 1970. Houston had departed in the summer of 1960.

4. For labels such as Foundry, Breadbasket, and Dixie *inter alia*, see Joel Garreau, *The Nine Nations of North America* (Boston: Houghton Mifflin, 1981).

5. The wording appears in the *Missouri Republican* of January 8, 1855, and is quoted in Richard C. Wade, *Slavery in the Cities: The South, 1820–1860* (New York: Oxford University Press, 1964), p. 15. More recently, Cincinnati was "as far South as you can get and still be in the North," according to civil rights activist Rev. Fred Shuttlesworth, who moved to Cincinnati in 1962. Bill Reynolds uses the phrase "more Southern than Midwestern" about Cincinnati in *Cousy: His Life, Career, and the Birth of Big-Time Basketball* (New York: Simon & Schuster, 2005), p. 255.

6. Classifying Tulsa is difficult. It claims to be the Oil Capital of the World, Houston's long lead notwithstanding, and people use the term Southwest in describing Tulsa. However, Tulsa can be classified as part of "the peripheral Midwest" according to Joseph W. Brownell, "The Cultural Midwest," *Journal of Geography*, vol. 59 (1960), p. 83, figure 2. Garreau

lists Oklahoma as "one of the more schizophrenic places on the continent," p. 342. Figuring out Denton is not easy, either, because the place is close to the Dallas-Fort Worth "metroplex," and therefore is a part of Dixie (Garreau, pp. 137–138). Yet, Denton is farm country; North Texas State football players have been called "oversize farmboys" (*Sports Illustrated*, September 18, 1961, p. 69). Raymond D. Gastil uses the term "Western South" in *Cultural Regions of the United States* (Seattle: University of Washington Press, 1975), p. 203. More about Dallas can be found in John Gunther, *Inside U.S.A.* (New York/London: Harper & Brothers, 1947), pp. 829–830.

7. The figures are for 1960 and are given in Lavinia P. Dudley and John J. Smith, eds., *The Americana Annual* (New York/Chicago/Washington, DC: Americana Corporation, 1961), pp. 155, 156, 157, 163, 168, and 167 respectively, except for the St. Louis figure which comes from Donald J. Hutter, ed., *Mirror of 150-Year Progress of the Catholic Church in the United States of America* (Cleveland: Mirror Publishing Company, 1964), p. 55. The numbers are perhaps inexact a bit, since another source lists the following enrollment figures: Bradley 3,300 students; Cincinnati 16,338; Drake 3,450; North Texas 6,779; St. Louis 7,797; Tulsa 6,000; and Wichita 6,500 (*Missouri Valley Conference All Sports Handbook for 1959–1960*, n.p., pp. 5–6).

8. Long after the establishment of Drake University, the Disciples of Christ counted among their members perhaps the greatest college basketball coach of all time, John Wooden, who labored for two seasons at Indiana State Teachers College (now University; 1946–1947 and 1947–1948, 44–15) and for 27 at the University of California at Los Angeles ([UCLA]; 1948–1949 to 1974–1975, 620–147). For some interesting details about Wooden, see John E. Miller, "Lawrence Welk and John Wooden: Midwestern Small-Town Boys Who Never Left Home," *Journal of American Studies*, vol. 38, no. 1 (April 2004), pp. 109–125.

9. For more information see John Jakle, "America's Small Town/Big City Dialectic," *Journal of Cultural Geography*, vol. 18

(Spring/Summer 1999), pp. 1–27. Further, see Timothy R. Mahoney, "The Small City in American History," *Indiana Magazine of History*, vol. 99, no. 4 (December 2003), pp. 311–330.

10. *Americana* (1961), pp. 485, 555, 377, 557, 401, 344, and 751.

11. There are connections between Tulsa and Peoria beyond basketball: they are both good test markets. See Steve Lohr, "Test It in Tulsa—It'll Play in Peoria," *Chicago Tribune*, June 7, 1992, sec. 7, p. 3.

12. The figure for Lawrence, Kansas is from *Americana* (1961), p. 401.

13. Oklahoma State (as Oklahoma A&M, of course) joined the Valley in the 1920's, but left it in 1957.

14. Today's Gateway Conference (on the 1-AA level) is the modern Valley football analogue. Former Valley members Cincinnati, North Texas, and Tulsa now play in Division 1-A, elsewhere. Drake today participates in the Pioneer League; St. Louis, Wichita State, and Bradley do not play either 1-A or 1-AA football. New Mexico State (1972–1973 until 1982–1983) and West Texas State (1971–1972 until 1984–1985; now West Texas A&M University) are remembered for playing men's basketball in the Valley, not so much for their contributions to Valley football. For more see Rebecca Jane Sankner, *The History of the Gateway Conference* (Ph.D. dissertation, Southern Illinois University, Carbondale, 1995).

15. Many will associate the name of Bradley University with some gambling scandals of the late 1940's and early 1950's. See Albert J. Figone, "Gambling and College Basketball: The Scandal of 1951," *Journal of Sport History*, vol. 16, no. 1 (Spring 1989), pp. 44–61; David C. Whelan, *Organized Crime, Sports Gambling and Role Conflict: Victimization and Point-Shaving in College Basketball* (Ph.D. dissertation, City University of New York, 1992), pp. 49–50; and Charles E. Quirk, ed., "Jack Molinas: A Basketball Player with Great But Unclean Hands," *Sports and the Law: Major Legal Cases* (New York: Garland Publishing, 1996), pp. 125–128. For a view of gambling today through the eyes of forensic economics see Justin Wolfers, "Point Shaving: Corruption in NCAA Basketball," *American Economic Review*, vol. 96, no. 2 (May 2006), pp. 279–283.

16. See Joe Jares, *Whatever Happened to Gorgeous George?* (New York: Grosset & Dunlap, 1974), p. 181. Kiel Auditorium, born in 1934, certainly would have made a wonderful place for a professional wrestling hall of fame, but it would have competition today from a room on the second floor of the Cincinnati Gardens, also a venue for Valley games. The University of Cincinnati played some of its games in the Gardens. Huge crowds were reported there against local rival Xavier University: 13,417 on March 1, 1962 and 14,133 on February 26, 1963. Those numbers are noteworthy since the building's capacity was 11,000 when it was built in 1949. Old Kiel Auditorium is now gone, having been replaced by the Kiel Center, which is now the Scottrade Center. Gone, too, is the St. Louis Arena (cap. 21,000), born five years before Kiel. The Arena in its day hosted practically everything: hockey, dairy exhibits, horse shows, college and professional basketball, professional wrestling, and you-name-it. St. Louis University also played men's varsity basketball in the Arena from 1968–1969 to 1972–1973, from 1978–1979 to 1981–1982, and from 1991–1992 to 1993–1994.

Chapter Two: The Power Increases, 1958–1960

1. The University of Houston participated in Valley athletics from 1951–1952 until 1959–1960, then dropped out. The school's membership explains why there were 14 league games in that 1959–1960 season, but a dozen in the 1960–1961 season. The figures shown on the three *Tables* that follow come from *Bradley Braves Basketball Press Guide, 2004–2005*, pp. 127–128; *Cincinnati Men's Basketball Media Guide, 2004–2005*, pp. 120–121; *Drake Media Guide, 2004–2005*, pp. 99–100; *The Yucca* (yearbook of North Texas State College), 1960 (pp. 165–172), 1961 (pp. 171–179), 1962 (pp. 177–185), 1963 (pp. 305–317), 1964 (pp. 341–351); *St. Louis Billikens Basketball Media Guide,*

2003–2004, pp. 120–121; *Tulsa 2003–2004 Men's Basketball Media Guide*, pp. 196–197; and *2005 [Wichita State University] Shocker Basketball Guide*, pp. 142–143.

2. Concerning John Benington, evidence seems to indicate that he was a very nice person. See Bruce Jenkins, *A Good Man: The Pete Newell Story* (Berkeley, CA: North Atlantic Books, 1999). The motion has been seconded by Jim Murray, Kiel Auditorium public address announcer for St. Louis University games between 1956 and 1958 (interview with author, Morris, Illinois, August 7, 2004). Newell and Benington collaborated on *Basketball Methods* (New York: Ronald Press Co., 1962). At sidebar, it should be noted that some schools were all but wedded to the NIT; Benington of St. Louis and Chuck Orsborn of Bradley never coached a game in the NCAA tournament. Ralph Miller of Wichita coached only two games in the NCAA tourney, both in 1964. Maurice John of Drake participated in the NIT in 1964, but not in the NCAA tournament until the spring of 1969.

3. Much has been written about Peoria. See Bryan J. Ogg, *Wish You Were Here: Peoria Edition* (Slinger, WI: Brandt Printing, Inc., 1997), and Anna Gregoline, "Heading West on I-74, Cresting the Hill with the Gas Tank on E, I return to the Land of Too Many Vowels," *Broadside* [Bradley University literary arts journal], vol. 20 (2001), p. 63. Visits to Peoria must have created vivid impressions years ago; Robertson Fieldhouse at Bradley was labeled the "Peorian snakepit" in the yearbook of the University of Cincinnati in 1964 (*The Cincinnatian*, p. 318). Further, serpents must have been plentiful in the Valley, since Drake's Maurice John called the Men's Gym at North Texas a snakepit in February, 1970 when his Bulldogs lost a double overtime game there.

4. "Missouri Valley," *Sports Illustrated*, December 7, 1959, p. 53. For some background about Benton Harbor, Michigan, where Walker grew up, see Alex Kotlowitz, *The Other Side of the River: A Story of Two Towns, a Death, and America's Dilemma* (New York: Nan A. Talese/Doubleday, 1998). Walker and his parents had moved from northern Mississippi to Benton Harbor.

Kotlowitz writes that Benton Harbor looks "as if someone had taken an inner-city neighborhood ... and plopped it in the middle of this otherwise picturesque landscape" (p. 4). Some may remember that Walker's Bethlehem, Mississippi is not that far from Money, Mississippi, the place where young Emmett Till was killed in 1955. George Will writes that the trip from northern Mississippi to Chicago (about 16 hours by Illinois Central train!) was costing $11.00 in 1955. See "'Men Stood Up Who Had Never Stood Up Before'," *Chicago Sun-Times*, June 19, 2005, p. 43A.

5. Jeremiah Tax, "A Mighty Roar in Peoria," *Sports Illustrated*, January 25, 1960, p. 19. In Robertson's book, *The Big O: My Life, My Times, My Game* (Emmaus, PA: Rodale Publishing, 2003), there is a mention of Jeremiah Tachs (pp. 105, 211. One reads Tax in Jenkins, p. 197. It is Tax in Robert Allen Cherry, *Wilt: Larger Than Life* (Chicago: Triumph Books, 2004), p. 54.

6. Some claim that the NIT tournament was simply a poor cousin to the NCAA tournament; such a judgment is perhaps too rapid. See Jeffrey L. Kessler, "Tournament Has Become March Monopoly Madness," *New York Times*, March 28, 2004, sec. 8, p. 10, as opposed to Dave Gavitt, "N.C.A.A. Pits the Best Against the Best," *New York Times*, April 4, 2004, p. 9. John Wooden takes an opposite stand, that is against the NIT's adequate nature, in Jenkins, pp. 50, 128, 224. The record shows that Wooden *never* coached a game in the NIT. Adolph Rupp coached only 11 games there in 42 years. Henry Iba coached only eight games in 41 years. Forrest C. "Phog" Allen of Kansas *never* coached a game there in almost four decades.

7. Walker (with Chris Messenger) has written *A Long Time Coming: A Black Athlete's Coming-of-Age in America* (New York: Grove Press, 1995). For more information on Walker and black life at Bradley see Arwin D. Smallwood, *Blacks at Bradley, 1897–2000* (Chicago: Arcadia Publishing, 2001).

8. Details about Mannie Jackson can be found in Dale Ratermann, *The Big Ten: A Century of Excellence* (Champaign, IL: Sagamore Publishing, 1996), p. 273.

Chapter Three: Bearcats Forever! 1960–1961

1. Electing a Catholic as President of the United States may have been more unlikely during the five-year period than having coaches in the national championship basketball game who have not been head coaches for very long. On the issue of President Kennedy, Valley fans who are historians will often say quickly that Mayor Richard J. Daley of Chicago "stole" the 1960 presidential election for John F. Kennedy. Maybe not. See "The Myth of 1960," *Chicago Tribune*, April 24, 2005, sec. 2, p. 10. Kennedy is remembered clearly for his statement to the Greater Houston Ministerial Association in September of 1960, "I do not speak for my church on public matters—and the church does not speak for me."

2. Fred Taylor and his Buckeyes were only 11–11 in 1958–1959, but appeared in three Final Fours in a row (1960, 1961, 1962). He was 297–158 (.653) overall. (Taylor also played 22 games in major league baseball for the Washington Senators.) And to think Cincinnati participated in five straight Final Fours (1959, 1960, 1961, 1962, 1963).

3. An interesting trivia question surrounds Carl Bouldin of Cincinnati. He is the only person to play in an NCAA championship game in men's basketball and also play major league baseball in the same year (1961). He took the mound for the Washington Senators in the fall of that year on September 2, about two weeks before his 22nd birthday. Some may mention Tim Stoddard of North Carolina State, who played in the NCAA men's basketball championship game on March 25, 1974 and later debuted in major league baseball on September 7, 1975 for the Chicago White Sox. He was born on January 24, 1953.

4. *Anaga* (1961), p. 133.

5. The venue for the first performance of "Willie Wampum" was the Milwaukee Arena (now U.S. Cellular Arena). The character was put away on April 1, 1971.

6. "Vinnie Ernst, 54, Record-Setter for Providence Basketball Team," *New York Times*, December 25, 1996, p. B9.

7. Slavin's Providence College was "open but not proactive" in recruiting black students and black athletes, to hear two Providence alumni tell it: Charles J. Sutter (class of 1965) and Francis W. Stripling (class of 1969) (interviews with author, Bogota, New Jersey, October 8, 2004). One source says that at Providence there were six blacks amid 1,200 students at the time when Len Wilkens was there in the late 1950's (Gary Smith, "He Overcame," *Sports Illustrated*, December 5, 1994, p. 71). For the record, one reads that there were 226 black students out of a student population of more than 30,000 in 1966 at the University of California (in Berkeley) according to Jenkins, p. 212.

8. Lemons was a master of the one-liner. He said to fellow Oklahoman Johnny Bench, a Major League Baseball Hall of Famer, "If you had come with me, you'd be a high school principal by now." Lemons frequently commented, "I don't jog. If I am going to die, I want to be sick first." On a serious note, Lemons was 74–58 at OCU between 1959–1960 and 1963–1964, and 309–181 overall there. (Neither Oklahoma nor Oklahoma State played OCU then, for the record.) Lemons also coached at the University of Texas, where he was 110–63 in six seasons. Athletic Director DeLoss Dodds at Texas called Lemons into his office after the 1981–1982 season and said, "You're fired." Lemons remarked that he looked around to see if anyone else was in the room.

9. Lambert to Mullins, November 19, 1960, "Missouri Valley Conference Membership, Correspondence and Information, 1950, 1956–1957, 1959–1961," Record Group B-2.1, Series 1, Box 2, Folder 1, Marquette University Department of Special Collections and University Archives. Marquette did not join the Valley. The school had announced on December 9, 1960 that football would be dropped; the decision may have had something to do with the school's unwillingness to go into the Valley. Further, according to the *Milwaukee Journal* of May 12, 1961, Athletic Director Mullins was being relieved of his duties as of January 31, 1962, a scant 13 months after the football announcement. Head basketball Coach Eddie Hickey took over as Athletic

Director. He lasted until April 3, 1964. Hickey was the school's eighth head basketball coach, and ended at Marquette with 92 wins and 70 losses after six seasons. He preceded Al McGuire, who went on to post a record of 295–80 in 13 seasons. Laboring at Marquette through three years of Hickey and all the years of McGuire was St. Louis University graduate Hank Raymonds, who himself became a successful head coach in Milwaukee, going 126–50 in the six seasons immediately after McGuire. Some may remember Hickey for his knowledge of the fast break, described in "St. Louis' Controlled Three-Lane Fast Break," *Scholastic Coach*, vol. 25, no. 4 (December 1955), pp. 10–11, 30–31.

Chapter Four: Bearcats Again! 1961–1962

1. The Reds played three games at home during the Series and lost all three. A packed house of only 32,589 attended each game at Crosley Field. Today the size of those crowds would generate an expression of sympathy. And to think there were 54,432 fans in attendance for the semifinal game in 2003 between Kansas and Marquette in New Orleans at the Superdome.

2. Bradley and the NIT were a nice fit for each other. See Dick Lien, "NIT: Ours, and Now We Just Love It," *Peoria Journal Star*, March 22, 1994, p. D1. There was a long interval for the Braves in the NCAA tournament; they played on March 12, 1955, but not again until March 7, 1980.

3. Issues of segregation and integration were not easy. See Ronald E. Marcello, "Reluctance versus Reality: The Desegregation of North Texas State College, 1954–1956," *Southwestern Historical Quarterly*, vol. 100, no. 2 (October 1996), pp. 153–185.

4. The home court advantage is discussed in Barry Schwartz and Stephen F. Barsky, "The Home Advantage," *Social Forces*, vol. 55, no. 3 (March 1977), pp. 641–661, as well as in Eldon E. Snyder and Dean A. Purdy, "The Home Advantage in Collegiate Basketball," *Sociology of Sport Journal*, vol. 2, no. 4 (December 1985), pp. 352–356.

5. Many numbers were important in the life of Wilt Chamberlain. See Gary M. Pomerantz, *Wilt 1962: The Night of 100 Points and the Dawn of a New Era* (New York: Crown Publishing Group, 2005).

Chapter Five: The Game, 1962–1963

1. Walter Bingham, "Life in the Valley of Death," *Sports Illustrated*, January 21, 1963, pp. 52–54. The "valley of death" phrase is also found in the yearbook of the University of Cincinnati in 1963, *The Cincinnatian*, p. 261.

2. John Underwood, "Cincy Goes for a Third," *Sports Illustrated*, March 11, 1963, pp. 24–29.

3. Perhaps Loyola was starting to creep back into the game because George Ireland had used IMPROVE-A-SHOT rims (U.S. patent No. 2,918,283) during Loyola practices. He once mentioned the devices to an inquiring young man about a month before Loyola won the championship (letter from Ireland to John P. Jursinic of Joliet, Illinois, February 20, 1963; on file with author). Ireland encouraged Jursinic to pursue the matter with IMPROVE-A-SHOT's developer, Paul M. Marschalk of Pierre, South Dakota. The devices were priced at $6.95 each.

4. Rush seemed synonymous years ago with Loyola basketball, and many will remember him yelling into the WCFL (AM 1000) microphone, "We won! We won! We won!" like a giddy child after the championship win over Cincinnati. See Joe Goddard, "Swisheroo! Ex-broadcaster Nothing But One Swella Fella," *Chicago Sun-Times*, February 27, 2005, p. 97A. The Loyola-Cincinnati game was bumped from Chicago-area television (WGN, Channel 9) by the Illinois High School Association (IHSA) game featuring the Carver High Challengers (with future Bradley star Joe Allen) against the Centralia High Orphans. Carver won, 53–52, on a shot by reserve Anthony Smedley who played a total of nine seconds! The *Chicago Tribune* blared the next day, "Loyola Rules U.S., Carver the State!" Some Chicagoans were watching WTTW, Channel 11 (Chicago), which was broadcasting

the Indiana High School Athletic Association (IHSAA) basketball championship from Butler (now Hinkle) Fieldhouse in Indianapolis at roughly the same hour that the Carver-Centralia game was played. The Muncie Central Bearcats defeated the South Bend Central Bears in another thriller, 65–61. For information on March Madness in Illinois, see Richard Sandomir, "What Are the Origins of Madness?," *New York Times*, March 25, 2005, p. C19.

5. *Pittsburgh Courier*, March 23, 1963, p. 15.

6. George Wilson thinks there may have been some strange calls during the game. See Goddard, "Memories of 'Ripoffs' Still Rile One of State's Greats," *Chicago Sun-Times*, March 27, 2005, p. 77A. Elsewhere, one hears little criticism of the two men who officiated, Bill Bussenius and Alex George. The former went on to work the 1966 and the 1968 Final Fours, among several other big games. The latter had worked the 1960 Final Four. Some fans from Cincinnati may have had other things on their minds on March 23, the day of the Loyola-Cincinnati game: there was the upcoming professional wrestling match involving William Frederick ("Dick the Bruiser") Afflis in the city on March 30! (Fans of rock 'n' roll music will recall that on that same day in New York City a high school junior, Leslie Gore, went into a Manhattan recording studio and produced "It's My Party"!)

7. Perhaps coaches at the time of the 1963 tournament had read Jucker's 1962 book (*Cincinnati Power Basketball* [Englewood Cliffs, NJ: Prentice-Hall]) as well as an article in a national magazine in 1961 (Ray Cave, "A Long-neglected Art is Now Flourishing Again," *Sports Illustrated*, February 6, 1961, pp. 48–50). He credits two West Coast coaches, Phil Woolpert at the University of San Francisco and Pete Newell at the University of California, for an emphasis on defensive skills. Again for the record, John Wooden used to speak extensively at basketball clinics, at least in the mid-1970's, about the importance of offense. On several occasions he would ask, "How many of you [coaches] spend more time coaching defense than you do on coaching offense?" A majority of the coaches in attendance would raise

their hands proudly. Wooden would respond dryly, "I would love to have you on my schedule." After a few seconds of silence, with coaches looking puzzled at each other, Wooden would patiently explain that coaching offense takes longer to teach than defense and takes longer to learn (than defense). (The author was present at a clinic on more than one occasion for Wooden's comments on this subject.) His thinking seems correct: the execution of offense (or the lack of said execution) is supremely important and determines most often the outcome of a game. While coaches everywhere will shout, "Defense wins championships," the statement seems to assume a fact not in evidence. A better phrasing might be, "Poorly executed offense loses championships." The emphasis on defense does seem to be a good motivational tool, but it is not the best answer to the question, "What determines outcomes of games?" Wooden backed up his lectures by putting on the floor teams that would attack the rim relentlessly from the opening jump ball until the final buzzer. Current basketball commentator and former UCLA great Bill Walton (1971–1972 until 1973–1974) often mentions Wooden's thinking on this topic. Walton has been known to groan on the air when seeing a team stall; he cannot understand, similar to Wooden, why a team does not attack the basket at all times. Wooden's own words on the subject can be found in his *Practical Modern Basketball*, 3rd ed. (New York: Ronald Press Co., 1966), p. 242. Further, this point may be more easily seen in a game of football, in which the team that has the ball longer usually wins. The team has the ball longer because it has a good running back. A good running attack in effect pins the other team against its goal line, thereby opening the door for a defensive unit to come on the field and do some good things, possibly against a team that may perform poorly on offense. Not to mention that offense "sells itself," and it does not need the promotional patter that playing defense and coaching defense does. Lastly, does any basketball recruiter rejoice about a prospect who can cling to his man like a blanket, but not sink a 12-foot jump shot from straight away? The final point comes from Dean Oliver, *Basketball on Paper: Rules and Tools for Performance Analysis* (Washington, DC: Brassey's, Inc., 2004), p. 141. In addition, some may wish to read Thomas Gilovich et al., "The Hot Hand in Basketball: On the Misperception of Random Sequences," *Cognitive Psychology*, vol. 17, no. 3 (1985), pp. 295–314, or Amos Tversky and Gilovich, "The Cold Facts About the 'Hot Hand' in Basketball," *Chance*, vol. 2, no. 1 (Winter 1989), pp. 16–21.

8. Jucker, in Jerry Krause and Ralph Pim, eds., *Coaching Basketball* (New York: Contemporary Books, 2002), p. 383. Perhaps Jucker's bias about defense took root in his desire to motivate his players, possibly because many of them, if not all of them, were recruited to Cincinnati for their ability to play offense.

9. From the opening tip there were issues of both basketball and race. See Ron Fimrite, "It Was More Than Just a Game," *Sports Illustrated*, November 18, 1987, pp. 106–115. Some coaches made the remark on the banquet circuit that Ireland was indeed a busy man since he was "in Africa—recruiting" (Richard Goldstein, "George Ireland, 88, Title-Winning Coach at Loyola, Dies," *New York Times*, September 20, 2001, p. A28).

10. Jucker went only 31–21 (17–9 and 14–12) in his last two years at Cincinnati, that is after the 1963 loss to Loyola. Once the duo of Tom Thacker and Tony Yates left, the going was much more difficult. Baseball fans may remember that Jucker crossed paths with baseball's Sandy Koufax at the University of Cincinnati. Koufax was not a bad basketball player as a Cincinnati student, and his skills in baseball were still being refined at the time. He averaged 9.7 points per game on the freshman basketball team, and was 3–1 on the mound with the Bearcats, sporting an earned run average of 2.81.

11. Another account of the events surrounding Wilson and his mates can be found in Underwood, "The Ramblers Wreck Cincy," *Sports Illustrated*, April 1, 1963, pp. 23–25, 82.

12. One must remember throughout that only the conference winner was invited to the NCAA tournament at the time. As

loaded as a team like Wichita was, it did not go to the NCAA tournament if it did not win the Valley title. Imagine what Bradley could have done if it had been invited to the tournament in addition to Cincinnati. Peorians can only dream. Some in the Atlantic Coast Conference (ACC) will recall a 1973–1974 Maryland team that went 23–5 overall, but lost, 103–100, in overtime in the ACC tournament final to eventual national champion North Carolina State (with the previously mentioned Stoddard). The Terrapins did not play one game after the ACC tournament.

Chapter Six: Great Times in Peoria, 1963–1964

1. Few may realize that former basketball coach George Raveling (Washington State, Iowa, and Southern California) possesses some of the notes used by Dr. King on that important day in 1963. Raveling was only a few steps away, and King made no effort to put the notes away in any safe place. He told Raveling that he may find them useful some day.

2. Sports and games took some interesting turns only hours after the Kennedy assassination. The Cleveland Browns of the National Football League hosted the Dallas Cowboys at Municipal Stadium in Cleveland, and the Cleveland fans booed the Dallas players when they took the field. It was, in the words of Dallas coach Tom Landry, "as if the events of that [Friday] afternoon had suddenly tainted everything having to do with Dallas, Texas" (Landry [with Gregg Lewis], *Tom Landry: An Autobiography* [Grand Rapids: Zondervan Publishing House, 1990], p. 147).

3. Coach John Jordan of Notre Dame in the late 1950's and early 1960's could speak of the difficulties of neutral courts. Jordan in his 13 years at Notre Dame faced Kentucky four times in Louisville, not in Lexington, and twice in Chicago, not in South Bend. He lost all six times by an average margin of 17 points.

4. Some Peorians who did not play for the Bradley Braves have found the bright lights of the public eye as tantalizing as the quiet nights of Central Illinois. Born in Peoria were Peter John Fulton Sheen (in 1895), James Edward Jordan (1896), Marian Driscoll ([Jordan]; 1898), and Charles James Correll (1890). They are better known as (Catholic) Bishop Fulton J. Sheen, "Fibber McGee," "Molly," and "Andy" (of the old *Amos 'n' Andy* episodes, produced between 1951 and 1953). Some may remember that Francis Dayle "Chick" Hearn (1916) worked in Peoria media in the 1950's before becoming famous as a basketball announcer in professional basketball. Comedian Richard Pryor (1940) was also a Peorian, as well as baseball Hall of Fame announcer Jack Brickhouse (1916). All came from the so-called "cradle of the crossover dribble" (Alexander Wolff, *Big Game, Small World: A Basketball Adventure* [New York: Warner Books, 2002], pp. 123–135). Peoria's very successful Amateur Athletic Union (AAU) teams in the 1960's deserve a quick mention, too.

5. "Bradley Crushes N. Mexico, 86–54, for 3rd NIT Title," *Chicago American*, March 22, 1964, sec. 6, p. 60. The Braves-Lobos game during the day may be a quick lesson in the importance of a slippery concept, status. Playing a game at night carries a greater status today, and the dollars paid by advertisers reflect same.

6. McGuire also spoke of the obligation "to chase the day," as opposed to letting it come to an individual. The term appeared on opening night at the one-person play called *McGuire*, Helfaer Theatre, Marquette University, Milwaukee, June 11, 2005. The play was written by sportscaster Dick Enberg.

7. That same issue of *Sports Illustrated* details not only Louisville's acceptance of black players, but also Minnesota's. One reads on the same page about Archie Clark, Louis Hudson, and Don Yates of the Golden Gophers: "All are Negroes; no Negro has ever before played varsity basketball at Minnesota" ("College Basketball, 1964," *Sports Illustrated*, December 9, 1963, p. 54). For the record, Adolph Rupp of Kentucky *did* try to recruit Wes Unseld out of Seneca High in Louisville (Red Auerbach and John Feinstein, *Let Me Tell You a Story: A Lifetime*

in the Game [New York: Little, Brown and Co., 2004], p. 86).
Unseld, however, adds, "They never seriously recruited me"
(Harvey Araton, "A Color Film. Story? Black and White.," *New
York Times*, January 12, 2006, p. C20). (Was Rupp the last coach
to go to the Final Four with an all-white team? Interestingly, no.
Dean Smith of North Carolina was the last in the spring of 1967.
The Tar Heels finished an unsatisfactory fourth there.)

Chapter Seven: The Days Dwindle, 1964–1965

1. Stallworth is also remembered for the heart attack that he
suffered during his professional career on March 7, 1967.

2. John McPhee, *A Sense of Where You Are: A Profile of
William Warren Bradley* (New York: Farrar, Straus, and Giroux,
1978). Both Wichita and Providence were blasted by Bill Bradley
and Princeton. Jimmy Walker of Providence, however, responded
to Princeton with 27 points of his own.

3. The bid was turned down by Bradley's Board of Trustees,
sparking the students to protest. See *Anaga* (1966), p. 149. Wichita
did go to the NIT, but lost in the first game to New York University.

4. John and Drake did the Valley proud in the Final Four in
1969. Drake almost defeated UCLA in Louisville, the same place
where Loyola had beaten Cincinnati in 1963. The UCLA-Drake
game is the most exciting game ever played to date by a Valley
team in the NCAA tournament.

5. The avuncular Wooden apparently was no perennial saint
on the sidelines, at least according to Jenkins who refers to "a
spicy brand of language that might have shocked his adoring fans"
(p. 121). Referee Weiler says that Wooden's talk was "vulgar, but
not to me" (telephone conversation with author, July 18, 2005).

6. Alcindor's school was Power Memorial Academy, administered by the Christian Brothers of Ireland, and the lone loss was
to powerful DeMatha High, also a Catholic school, but run by
the Trinitarians in Hyattsville, Maryland. The score was 46–43 at
Cole Field House on the campus of the University of Maryland on
January 30, 1965 before 12,500 fans.

7. The point is made by Joe Menzer, *Four Corners: How UNC, N.C. State, Duke, and Wake Forest Made North Carolina the Center of the Basketball Universe* (Lincoln, NE: University of Nebraska Press, 2004), p. 147. Recent Tar Heel media guides say little about Cooper.

Chapter Eight: Below the Surface

1. John T. McGreevy, "Thinking on One's Own: Catholicism in the American Intellectual Imagination, 1929–1960," *Journal of American History*, vol. 84, no. 1 (June 1997), p. 130. In the same vein, see Lawrence H. Fuchs, *John F. Kennedy and American Catholicism* (New York: Meredith Press, 1967), pp. 182–188.

2. Pat Conroy says that one does not have to tell the whole world about playing against inferior opponents. One should recite the names of tougher ones on the schedule. In conversation he would bypass a mention of schools like Wofford, Presbyterian, and Erskine, but include a mention of Auburn, Florida State, and Virginia Tech! (*My Losing Season* [New York: Bantam, 2002], p. 33).

3. Memphis State was a Valley member from 1967–1968 until 1972–1973. The team made the Final Four in 1973, but lost to UCLA in the championship game.

4. Some tranquil days in St. Louis are described in Kenneth Jolly, *It Happened Here Too: The Black Liberation Movement in St. Louis, Missouri, 1964–1970* (Ph.D. dissertation, University of Missouri, Columbia, 2003). For a brief mention of St. Louis and a large mention of desegregation, see Jonathan Guryan, "Desegregation and Black Dropout Rates," *American Economic Review*, vol. 94, no. 4 (September 2004), p. 927.

5. Bingham, p. 54. Perhaps Coach Harp was bitter because Oscar Robertson and Cincinnati had defeated Harp's Jayhawks in an NCAA regional game in 1960, 82–71, in which Robertson scored 43 points and gathered 14 rebounds. Harp's perspective may have been shaped, too, by Wilt Chamberlain leaving Kansas in 1958 for work with the Harlem Globetrotters. Wilt was paid per year somewhere between $46,000 (John Taylor, *The Rivalry:*

Bill Russell, Wilt Chamberlain, and the Golden Age of Basketball [New York: Random House, 2005], p. 103) and $65,000 (Pomerantz, p. 45). Ben Green mentions "a base salary of $46,000" (*Spanning the Globe: The Rise, Fall, and Return to Greatness of the Harlem Globetrotters* [New York: HarperCollins, 2005], p. 291). Cherry says the number is $65,000 (p. 99). Maybe Harp was thinking of his own Final Four participation as a Kansas player (27 points in three games) in 1940; skilled black players were not seen anywhere then. Harp should not be roundly condemned; he supposedly did not care for "a quota system" in place when he was at Kansas as head coach (Jack Olsen, "Part II: The Black Athlete," *Sports Illustrated*, July 8, 1968, p. 30).

6. Joe Stowell, interview with author, Peoria, Illinois, October 29, 2004.

7. Smith, "Moment of Truth," *Sports Illustrated*, July 26, 1999, p. 149.

8. Andrew Sullivan, "What We Look Up to Now," *New York Times Magazine*, November 15, 1998, sec. 6, p. 60.

Chapter Nine: And Below That...

1. For an introduction about what is said and not said racially see Cheryl Glenn, *Unspoken: A Rhetoric of Silence* (Carbondale, IL: Southern Illinois University Press, 2004), pp. xx-xxi.

2. William I. Thomas, *The Child in America: Behavior Problems and Programs* (New York: A. A. Knopf, 1928), p. 572. Thomas makes two contributions on that same page. He speaks of things being "real in their consequences," and also uses "as if," the tiny conjunction whose dimensions may explain some of the black-white relation. Thomas writes of an occasional situation "which may be in terms of objective reality or in terms of a subjective appreciation—'as if' it were so."

3. The story that is multiculturalism seems at times very weak. See Murray L. Wax, "The Irrelevance of Multiculturalism," *Sociological Imagination*, vol. 32, no. 2 (1995), pp. 119–125, as well as Jean S. Phinney, "When We Talk About American Ethnic

Groups, What Do We Mean?," *American Psychologist*, vol. 51, no. 9 (September 1996), pp. 918–927.

4. Lani Guinier, "From Racial Liberalism to Racial Literacy: *Brown v. Board of Education* and the Interest-Divergence Dilemma," *Journal of American History*, vol. 91, no. 1 (June 2004), p. 116.

5. Alfred Schutz, *On Phenomenology and Social Relations* (Chicago: University of Chicago Press, 1970), pp. 88, 89, 120. Some may recall herein Emile Durkheim's "collective representations" (and "collective effervescence"?).

6. For details see Frank Fitzpatrick, *And The Walls Came Tumbling Down: Kentucky, Texas Western, and the Game That Changed American Sports* (New York: Simon & Schuster, 1999). Interestingly, UCLA was the defending NCAA champion, and went a respectable 18–8 during the 1965–1966 season, but did not go to either the NCAA or the NIT tournaments. Oregon State represented the Athletic Association of Western Universities (AAWU). Perhaps UCLA wanted to stay at home to monitor the progress of freshman (Ferdinand) Lewis Alcindor. Further, Bruins coach John Wooden was no fan of the NIT; see Chapter Two, footnote 6 herein.

7. Michael Omi and Howard Winant, *Racial Formation in the United States: From the 1960's to the 1990's* (New York: Routledge, 1994), p. 165.

8. bell hooks speaks of another "double nature," that of being black and female, in *Ain't I a Woman?: Black Women and Feminism* (Boston: South End Press, 1984), p. 8. For another mix, that of black and Catholic (that is, black first, Catholic second), see James H. Cone, "Black Liberation Theology and Black Catholics: A Critical Conversation," *Theological Studies*, vol. 61, no. 4 (December 2000), p. 742. Cone developed the term "Black theology" in 1969. To paraphrase Cynthia Epstein, being black and female (or black and Catholic, for that matter) is one of the most cumulatively limiting of all the negatively evaluated statuses. Further, some associate the term "Black Power" with Stokely Carmichael in the Mississippi Delta on June 16, 1966. Historians might recall that Pierre Toussaint was both a slave and a Catholic.

9. Donald Spivey and Thomas A. Jones, "Intercollegiate Athletic Servitude: A Case Study of the Black Illini Student-Athletes, 1931–1967," *Social Science Quarterly*, vol. 55, no. 4 (March 1975), p. 945.

10. Carbondale is located in Dixie, to stay with the categories of Garreau, not in the Breadbasket or the slippery "Midwest." Humorists will add that Chicagoans believe that "Downstate" (Central and Southern Illinois combined) starts somewhere south of 111th Street in the city itself.

11. For more details see Diane McWhorter, *A Dream of Freedom: The Civil Rights Movement from 1954–1968* (New York: Scholastic, 2004).

12. See Declan Haun's photo, Civil Rights Supporters at the March in Washington for Jobs and Freedom, Washington, DC, 1963 (ICHi-36739), in *A Compassionate Eye: The Photographs of Declan Haun, 1961–1969*, Chicago Historical Society, October 9, 2004 through March 13, 2005. Too, smiling faces are seen in March of 1962 as Mayor Richard M. Daley of Chicago presented a key to James Weston and family to one of the Robert Taylor homes (at 5135 S. Federal Street) in Plate 50 of *The Promise of Public Housing, 1936–1983*, Gage Gallery, Roosevelt University, Chicago, January 31, 2005 through March 11, 2005. Things at the Taylor homes, however, went sour over the ensuing years. See Leslie Baldacci, "Lives Lost, Dreams Killed at 'Warehouse of the Poor,'" *Chicago Sun-Times*, January 7, 2006, p. 2. A similar history is found at Stateway Gardens, 3651-3653 S. Federal Street. Major league baseball's Kirby Puckett (1960–2006) at one time lived in the Taylor homes on Chicago's South Side at 4444 S. State Street. He played on the college level at Triton (Junior) College in River Grove, Illinois and at Bradley. His number (14) is retired at Bradley. A different number of his (34) has been retired by major league baseball's Minnesota Twins.

13. An excellent article on Crispus Attucks High in Indianapolis is that of Aram Goudsouzian, "Ba-ad, Ba-a-ad Tigers: Crispus Attucks Basketball and Black Indianapolis in the

1950's," *Indiana Magazine of History*, vol. 96, no. 1 (March 2000), pp. 5–43. For the record, Attucks High in Indianapolis was opened in 1927, was banned from state tournament play until 1943, and was integrated by court order in 1970. The high school of the same name in Carbondale, Illinois was organized in 1920, but was closed in 1964. These days some in Carbondale still remember the Blue Birds.

14. For all the talk of African-Americans in college basketball, college football may find itself in more dire straits on the subject of minority hiring and employment. Only one black who has been fired from a Division 1-A head coaching position has ever been hired for another (i.e., Tyrone Willingham, from Notre Dame to the University of Washington in 2004). And no team which has fired an African-American head coach has ever hired another one in his place. See Lynn Zinser, "Sylvester Croom, a Son of Alabama, Is Now a Rival," *New York Times*, July 18, 2004, sec. 8, pp. 1 and 7, and Malcolm Moran, "Croom All about Fixing Miss. State," *USA Today*, July 29, 2004, p. 3C. As of January 11, 2007, only seven black head coaches were found in Division 1-A football: Willingham, Karl Dorrell at UCLA, Croom, Ron Prince of Kansas State, Mario Cristobal at Florida International, Randy Shannon at Miami of Florida, and Turner Gill at the University of Buffalo. That is seven out of 119. A favorite quote in this intersection of sports and race was delivered by football coach Paul William "Bear" Bryant of Alabama on September 12, 1970. He said about running back Sam Cunningham of Southern California, "He did more for integration in the South in sixty minutes than Martin Luther King did in twenty years" (Richard E. Lapchick, *Five Minutes to Midnite: Race and Sport in the 1990's* [Lanham, MD: Madison Books, 1991], p. 227). For more on race and football in Alabama see Keith Dunnavant, *The Missing Ring: How Bear Bryant and the 1966 Alabama Crimson Tide Were Denied College Football's Most Elusive Prize* (New York: Thomas Dunne Books/St. Martin's Press, 2006). Dunnavant mentions that there were only 298

African American students at Alabama in 1966 (p. 88). A quote for the ages about football is that of Andrew D. White, president of Cornell University, who remarked in 1873 (upon considering his students going to play Michigan), "I will not permit thirty men to travel 400 miles merely to agitate a bag of wind."

15. Walter M. Abbott, S.J., ed., *The Documents of Vatican II* (New York: Guild Press, 1966), p. 267.

16. The sound of "black music" may have been moving between the harsh and the soft in the late 1960's and early 1970's. The soft side is heard in the Stylistics' recording of "You Are Everything" (Avco 4581, August 1971) and "Betcha by Golly, Wow" (Avco 4591, January 1972), to say nothing of the work of the Delfonics, or of Harold Melvin and the Blue Notes. Those soft (Philadelphia) sounds were counterbalanced at the time by Richard Roundtree as detective John Shaft in 1971. Yet to hear Gerald Early tell it, music from Detroit ("Motown") was "too white." Politically, new forms were emerging as the Civil Rights movement was encountering the Black Power Movement, born in 1966.

17. Charles H. Martin, "The Color Line in Midwestern College Sports, 1890–1960," *Indiana Magazine of History*, vol. 98, no. 2 (June 2002), pp. 95, 96, 97, 100, 108; "Racial Change and 'Big-Time' College Football in Georgia: The Age of Segregation, 1892–1957," *Georgia Historical Quarterly*, vol. LXXX, no. 3 (Fall 1996), pp. 537, 549, 550; "The Rise and Fall of Jim Crow in Southern College Sports: The Case of the Atlantic Coast Conference," *North Carolina Historical Review*, vol. 76, no. 3 (July 1999), p. 256; and "Integrating New Year's Day: The Racial Politics of College Bowl Games in the American South," in Patrick B. Miller, ed., *The Sporting World of the Modern South* (Urbana, IL: University of Illinois Press, 2002), p. 187. The exact number of blacks varied. Some schools were terrified to play one; others indeed played one. Some played two; a few institutions played three, etc. Loyola's Jerry Harkness, a black, has said that there was "an unwritten rule," allowing two blacks at most to play ("Chicago Tonite," WTTW, Channel 11 [Chicago]), March

30, 2005). One sportswriter says that the rule stipulated "two blacks at home, three on the road" (Bill Jauss, "Loyola's Dramatic Championship in '63 Tops City's Tournament Memories," *Chicago Tribune*, March 21, 1993, sec. 3, p. 9). Coach Don Haskins (with Dan Wetzel) gives the same formula (two blacks at home, three on the road) in *Glory Road: My Story of the 1966 NCAA Basketball Championship and How One Team Triumphed Against the Odds and Changed America Forever* (New York: Hyperion, 2006), p. 8, although the 2006 movie of the same name contains a different wording, that of "one at home, two on the road, three if you're losing." An entire chapter is given to the "gentleman's [*sic*] agreement" in Tom Graham and Rachel Graham Cody, *Getting Open: The Unknown Story of Bill Garrett and the Integration of College Basketball* (New York: Simon & Schuster, 2006), pp. 101–108. Putting three and four black players on the court at one time took place as far back as 1955 at Quincy College (now University) in Quincy, Illinois. See Steve Eighinger, "Only the Net Was White," *Quincy Herald-Whig*, April 17, 2005 at *www.whig.com/32603148444490.php*.

    18. Others have mentioned the gentlemen's agreement, too: Roy Wilkins, "That Old Southern Accent," in David K. Wiggins and Miller, eds., *The Unlevel Playing Field: A Documentary History of the African American Experience in Sport* (Urbana, IL: University of Illinois Press, 2003), p. 190; Jack Isenhauer, *Same Knight, Different Channel: Basketball Legend Bob Knight at West Point and Today* (Washington, DC: Brassey's, 2003), pp. 148–149; Timothy Davis, "The Myth of the Superspade: The Persistance of Racism in College Athletics," *Fordham Urban Law Journal*, vol. 22, no. 3 (Spring 1995), p. 627; Wiggins, *Glory Bound: Black Athletes in a White America* (Syracuse, NY: Syracuse University Press, 1997), pp. 68, 97; Russell J. Henderson, "The 1963 Mississippi State University Basketball Controversy and the Repeal of the Unwritten Law: 'Something more than the game will be lost,'" *Journal of Southern History*, vol. LXIII, no. 4 (November 1997), p. 828; David Wolf, *Foul:*

The Connie Hawkins Story (New York: Warner Paperback Library Edition, 1972), pp. 158–159; Randy Roberts, *'But They Can't Beat Us': Oscar Robertson and the Crispus Attucks Tigers* (Champaign, IL: Sports Publishing Inc., 1999), p. 176; and Ray Wolters, *New Negro On Campus: Black College Rebellions of the 1920's* (Princeton, NJ: Princeton University Press, 1975), pp. 316–317. John Sayle Watterson speaks of "a covenant of white supremacy" in *College Football: History, Spectacle, Controversy* (Baltimore: Johns Hopkins University Press, 2000), p. 310, while former Bradley assistant Chuck Buescher (1971–1972 until 1978–1979) mentions "a quota of one [black player] a year or one per team" (Dave Reynolds, "BU Moved Closer to Valley Than Hilltop During 1970's," at *www.pjstar.com/sports/ssections/teamofdecade/1971-1980.shtml*). Taylor adds that college coaches used "one black player at a time" (p. 60), and mentions that the NBA's Bill Russell had been mentioned by Milton Gross in the *New York Post* of April 18, 1966, saying that "a quota system" was in place in professional basketball (p. 271). Further, on the professional level, James Michener mentions "two blacks at home, three on the road, and five when you're eighteen points behind" (*Sports in America* [New York: Random House, 1976], p. 148). Taylor Branch uses the word "etiquette," that called for "no more than three" (*At Canaan's Edge: America in the King Years, 1965–1968* [New York: Simon & Schuster, 2006], p. 449). In the matter of football, Charles K. Ross writes of a time seven decades ago, "Although there is no written evidence of a 'gentlemen's agreement' between the owners, clearly there was unity between all NFL owners to keep black players out of the league" (*Outside the Lines: African Americans and the Integration of the National Football League* [New York: New York University Press, 1999], p. 79).

19. Martin, "Jim Crow in the Gymnasium: The Integration of College Basketball in the American South," in Wiggins and Miller, eds., *Sport and the Color Line: Black Athletes and Race Relations in Twentieth-century America* (New York: Routledge,

2004), p. 237. Martin also mentions the gentlemen's agreement (pp. 235, 237). This situation may remind some of Andrew Hacker's phrase "benign quotas" (*Two Nations: Black and White, Separate, Hostile, Unequal* [New York: Scribner's, 1992], p. 36).

20. Clarence "Sonny" Means, interview with author, Joliet, Illinois, October 19, 2004.

21. Stowell, interview, October 29, 2004.

22. Weiler, *ibid.*

23. It seems that Valley officials tried to ignore the black-white nature of the episode, to say nothing of its violence. A place to start to investigate the 1951 game involving Oklahoma State and Drake (with Johnny Bright) is found at *www.library.okstate.edu/ scua/PresPapers.htm.* Further, similar to the triumvirate of Means, Stowell, and Weiler, Drake historian Paul Morrison did not quickly conclude that Valley teams were avoided for issues of race; getting shellacked on the scoreboard may have been the reason (telephone conversation with author, April 14, 2005). Former coach Rick Majerus (Marquette, Ball State, Utah), when asked of the gentlemen's agreement, steered the question to details surrounding Babe "Magnolia Mouth" McCarthy, the head coach at Mississippi State (1955–1956 until 1964–1965) and his efforts to bring in black players to the school (conversation with author, Joliet, IL, June 23, 2006).

24. For a more disturbing look at some of the activities surrounding college basketball today, see Monifa Thomas, "Jackson Says NCAA Exploits Blacks," *Chicago Sun-Times,* March 26, 2005, p. 8.

Chapter Ten: Some Things Unfold

1. For talk about racism that is "aversive," see Paula S. Rothenberg, ed., *Race, Class and Gender in the United States: An Integrated Study* (New York: St. Martin's Press, 1992), p. 134.

2. Pardon E. Tillinghast, *The Specious Past: Historians and Others* (Reading, MA: Addison-Wesley, 1972), p. 4.

3. Walter Jost and Michael J. Hyde, eds., *Rhetoric and Hermeneutics in Our Time: A Reader* (New Haven/London: Yale University Press, 1997), p. xviii.

4. Eric Havelock, *Preface to Plato: A History of the Greek Mind* (Cambridge, MA: Belknap Press of Harvard University Press, 1963), p. vii. Further, one reads on the subject: "Sight, according to my judgment, has been the cause of the greatest blessing to us, inasmuch as of our present discourse concerning the universe not one word would have been uttered had we never seen the stars and the sun and the heavens" (R. D. Archer-Hind, ed., *The Timaeus of Plato* [New York: Arno Press, 1973], p. 163).

5. Mary R. Jackman, *The Velvet Glove: Paternalism and Conflict in Gender, Class, and Race Relations* (Berkeley, CA: University of California Press, 1994), p. 137.

6. Barbara J. Flagg, "'Was Blind But Now I See': White Race Consciousness and the Requirement of Discriminatory Intent," *Michigan Law Review*, vol. 91, no. 5 (March 1993), pp. 953–1017.

7. Robert J. Sampson and Stephen W. Raudenbush, "Seeing Disorder: Neighborhood Stigma and the Social Construction of 'Broken Windows'," *Social Psychology Quarterly*, vol. 67, no. 4 (2004), pp. 319–342. For more on broken windows, see Bernard E. Harcourt, *Illusion of Order: The False Promise of Broken Windows Policing* (Cambridge, MA: Harvard University Press, 2001), pp. 88–89.

8. Stephen Pentak and Richard Roth, *Color Basics* (Belmont, CA: Thomson/Wadsworth, 2004), p. 4.

9. Patricia J. Williams, *Seeing a Color-Blind Future: The Paradox of Race* (New York: Farrar, Straus and Giroux, 1997), p. 6. Is it ridiculous to ask what it is that blind people do not see? Forms and movement are two easy answers, but there seems to be more. Interaction (in its many meanings) may be another answer. In a differing way, one might ask if sighted people are also unable to see certain things that are not haptic, like talent or selfishness? The blind/sighted relation takes on an interesting side in New York's Theater By the Blind. See *www.tbtb.org*. Are not blind people compelled to live at times in a world of "as if"?

10. George Yancy, ed., *What White Looks Like: African-American Philosophers on the Whiteness Question* (New York: Routledge, 2004), p. 13. He has also edited *White on White/Black on Black* (Lanham, MD: Rowman & Littlefield Publishers, 2005).

11. Alex M. Johnson, Jr., "Bid Whist, Tonk, and *United States v. Fordice*: Why Integrationism Fails African-Americans Again," *California Law Review*, vol. 81, no. 6 (December 1993), pp. 1466–1467.

12. Some may notice Oprah lacking punctuality on occasion. See Mary Mitchell, "In Paris, Not Even Oprah Can Escape Reality of Being Black," *Chicago Sun-Times*, July 3, 2005, p. 14A. The issue was resolved with an apology from the people at Hermès (Alessandra Stanley, "Oprah, No Diva She, Accepts an Apology from Hermès," *New York Times*, September 20, 2005, p. C22).

13. Some mentions of color not easily associated with African-Americans are found in Kathy Russell et al., *The Color Complex: The Politics of Skin Color Among African Americans* (New York: Anchor Books, 1993).

14. Part of the puzzling prism of race is explained in D. Marvin Jones, "Darkness Made Visible: Law, Metaphor, and the Racial Self," *Georgetown Law Review*, vol. 82, no. 2 (December 1993), pp. 488–489.

15. Alva Noë, Action in Perception (Cambridge, MA: MIT Press, 2004), p. 96. Joseph Pieper also notes that seeing is an act of aggression in *Leisure: the Basis of Culture* (New York: New American Library, Inc., 1963), p. 25.

16. Michael T. Taussig, *Defacement: Public Secrecy and the Labor of the Negative* (Stanford, CA: Stanford University Press, 1999), p. 116.

17. A reduced ability to see did not happen years ago and then vanish. Today foreign language training is in dismal shape, pleasant talk to the contrary notwithstanding. Linguistic affairs, beyond a smattering of Spanish, are seen to be unimportant. The lack of contested terrain in the issue may be caused by a partial blindness. See Andrew Dalby, *Language in Danger: The Loss of Linguistic Diversity and the Threat to Our Future* (London/New York: Allen Lane, 2002), pp. 184–187.

18. Some may recall here Durkheim's term "renovated rationalism."

19. William B. Swann, Jr., "Identity Negotiation: Where Two Roads Meet," *Journal of Personality and Social Psychology*, vol. 53, no. 6 (December 1987), p. 1039.

20. Early, "Waiting for Miss America," in Elwood Watson and Darcy Martin, eds., *'There She is, Miss America': The Politics of Sex, Beauty, and Race in America's Most Famous Pageant* (New York: Palgrave Martin, 2004), pp. 180–183.

21. Thin-slicing is found in Gladwell, *Blink: The Power of Thinking Without Thinking* (New York: Little, Brown and Company, 2005), p. 23.

22. Some spoke of having to penetrate a "closed club" (Robert L. Green et al., "Blacks in the Big Ten," *Integrated Education*, vol. 10, no. 3 [May–June 1972], p. 36).

23. Pentak and Roth, *ibid.*

24. The point is made by Wiggins, "Prized Performers, but Frequently Overlooked Students: The Involvement of Black Athletes in Intercollegiate Sports on Predominantly White University Campuses, 1890–1972," *Research Quarterly for Exercise and Sport*, vol. 62, no. 2 (1991), p. 172. The elimination of racism by 1950 is also mentioned in Davis, *ibid.*, footnote 53.

25. Harry Edwards in Wolf, p. 85. The quote also appears in Olsen, "The Black Athlete—A Shameful Story," *Sports Illustrated*, July 1, 1968, p. 16.

26. Walker, p. 72.

27. Walker, p. 79.

28. W. E. B. Du Bois, *The Souls of Black Folks* (New York: Fawcett World Library, 1961), pp. 16–17.

29. King-To Yeung and John Levi Martin, "The Looking Glass Self: An Empirical Test and Elaboration," *Social Forces*, vol. 81, no. 3 (March 2003), p. 843. For more on

Cooley's looking glass see David C. Lundgren, "Social Feedback and Self-Appraisals: Current Status of the Mead-Cooley Hypothesis," *Symbolic Interaction*, vol. 27, no. 2 (Spring 2004), pp. 267–286.

30. The point is made by Early, "Performance and Reality," in Wiggins and Miller, p. 434.

31. Lisa J. McIntyre, *Law in the Sociological Enterprise: A Reconstruction* (Boulder, CO: Westview Press, 1994), p. 62.

32. Davis, p. 624.

33. For more details see Justine Coupland, "Small Talk: Social Functions," *Research on Language and Social Interaction*, vol. 36, no. 1 (2003), pp. 1–6.

Chapter Eleven: On a Philosophical Note

1. "As if" is an omnipresent item. It figures into religion: "Catholics acted [years ago] as if they had all the answers to the problems confronting mankind" (Charles E. Curran, *A New Look at Christian Morality* [Notre Dame, IN: Fides Publishers, 1970], p. 18). Too, abortion is talked about "as if it were as morally trivial as a tooth extraction" (Sullivan, "The Case for Compromise on Abortion," *Time*, March 7, 2005, p. 90). "As if" also finds a place in the world of psychology: "'As if' persons seem to have vivid interior lives" (Jay Martin, *Who Am I This Time?: Uncovering the Fictive Personality* [New York: Norton, 1988], p. 131). And the existence of God may require that humans live "as if God were not a straightforward given" (William Stacy Johnson, "Probing the Meaning of September 11, 2001," *The Princeton Seminary Bulletin*, vol. 23, no. 1 [February 2002], p. 45). In matters of science, one should read "A Philosophy of 'As If'" (R.I.M. Dunbar, *The Trouble With Science* [Cambridge, MA: Harvard University Press, 1995], p. 97). John Updike wrote that Ted Williams ran the bases after hitting the ball over the fence "as if our praise were a storm of rain to get out of." Chet Walker has written that Bradley's Joe Stowell once showed up at Walker's doorstep on a recruiting mission "as if summoned from a dream" (Walker, p. 60). For the basis of "as if" see Hans Vaihinger, *The Philosophy of 'As If,' A System of the Theoretical, Practical and Religious Fictions of Mankind*, trans. C. K. Ogden (New York: Harcourt, Brace and Company, 1925), p. 91. Interestingly, Williams uses "as though" fifteen times and "as if" once in her book.

2. Vaihinger, p. 93. For more about Vaihinger, see Heinrich Franz Wolf, *Philosophy for the Common Man* (New York: Philosophical Library, 1951).

3. Robertson speaks of himself being treated "as if I were a show pony about to do tricks" (Robertson, p. 86). Taylor says of the early days in the NBA, "It was not as if the owners had sat down and worked out a secret agreement to restrict black players" (p. 109). On the contrary, the owners might have. Decades ago some NBA executives voted to have a "rule" about black participation (Ron Thomas, *They Cleared the Lane* [Lincoln, NE: University of Nebraska Press, 2002], p. 25).

4. Robertson, p. 120.

5. William I. Thomas is not the only person to mention two significant things in one book on the same page. Richard H. Brown combines the looking glass theory and "as if" in *A Poetic for Sociology: Toward a Logic of Discovery for the Human Sciences* (Cambridge [Eng.]/New York: Cambridge University Press, 1977), p. 110.

6. The point is developed by Sandra Blakeslee, "What Other People Say May Change What You See," *New York Times*, June 28, 2005, p. D3.

7. Early, *Culture of Bruising: Essays on Prizefighting, Literature, and Modern American Culture* (Hopewell, NJ: Ecco Press, 1994), pp. 120–121.

8. Vaihinger, *Kant—Ein Metaphysiker?* (n.p., n.d. [detached from Sigwart-Festschrift]), p. 147.

9. The term is found in Margaret Jane Radin, "Property and Personhood," *Stanford Law Review*, vol. 34, no. 5 (May 1982), p. 963. See, too, Kevin Gray, "Property in Thin Air," *Cambridge Law Journal*, vol. 50, no. 2 (July 1991), pp. 252–307, and Cheryl

I. Harris, "Whiteness as Property" *Harvard Law Review*, vol. 106, no. 8 (June 1993), pp. 1709–1791.

Conclusion

1. Todd Boyd, *Young, Black, Rich, and Famous: The Rise of the NBA, the Hip Hop Invasion and the Transformation of American Culture* (New York: Doubleday, 2003), p. 14.

2. Walker, p. 73.

3. Today's research about Peoria and its black population can still hold one in thrall, especially when looking at voting patterns over the years. See James E. Loewen, *Sundown Towns: A Hidden Dimension of American Racism* (New York: W. W. Norton, 2005), pp. 148–149.

4. The opinion is that of Coach Rick Pitino of Louisville expressed in Joe Drape, "Geography is Destiny: Big East is the Best in the Land," *New York Times*, November 27, 2005, sec. 8, p. 5. Opinions that celebrated the Valley's standing on the national scene in 2006 are found in John Branch, "In the Hidden Heartland, a Claim on the Spotlight," *New York Times*, February 21, 2006, pp. C14–C15; Tim Wendel, "Things Are Looking Up in Missouri Valley," *USA Today*, March 3, 2006, pp. 1C–2C; Stewart Mandel, "Valley Boys," *Sports Illustrated*, February 20, 2006, pp. 48, 50; and Vic Reato, "High Peaks in Mo Valley," *Joliet [IL] Herald-News*, December 15, 2006, p. C1.

5. An explanation of life as a mid-major, a bad category on a good day, can be found in Bob Cook, "Four Mid-majors in Sweet 16? No surprise," at *www.msnbc.msn.com/id/11916225*. The confusing term seems to have come from Jack Kvanz, George Washington athletic director, in the *Washington Post* in 1977, at least according to Grant Wahl, "Once Upon a Time," *Sports Illustrated*, March 27, 2006, p. 42.

6. James P. Ronda in W. Raymond Wood, *Prologue to Lewis and Clark: The Mackay and Evans Expedition* (Norman, OK: The University of Oklahoma Press, 2003), p. xii.

Additional Reading

Adler, Patricia A. and Peter. *Backboards and Blackboards: College Athletes and Role Engulfment* (New York: Columbia University Press, 1991).

Allen, Theodore W. *The Invention of the White Race* (London/New York: Verso, 1994).

Anderson, Terry H. *The Movement and the Sixties: Protest in America from Greensboro to Wounded Knee* (New York: Oxford University Press, 1995).

Arnesen, Eric. *Black Protest and the Great Migration: A Brief History with Documents* (Boston: Bedford/St. Martin's, 2003).

Arsenault, Raymond. *Freedom Riders: 1961 and the Struggle for Racial Justice* (New York: Oxford University Press, 2006).

Ashburn-Nardo, Leslie et al. "Black Americans' Implicit Racial Associations and Their Implications for Intergroup Judgment," *Social Cognition*, vol. 21, no. 1 (February 2003), pp. 61–87.

Babchuk, Nicholas and Ralph V. Thompson. "The Voluntary Association of Negroes," *American Sociological Review*, vol. 27, no. 5 (October 1962), pp. 647–655.

Bal, Mieke. "Visual Essentialism and the Object of Visual Culture," *journal of visual culture*, vol. 2, no. 1 (April 2003), pp. 5–32.

Bartley, Numan V. *The New South, 1945–1980* (Baton Rouge, LA: Louisiana State University Press, 1995).

Bell, Derrick A. *Silent Covenants:* Brown v. Board of Education *and the Unfulfilled Hopes for Racial Reform* (New York: Oxford University Press, 2004).

Bell, Taylor. *Sweet Charlie, Dike, and Bobby Joe: High School Basketball in Illinois* (Urbana, IL: University of Illinois Press, 2004).

_____. *Glory Days Illinois: Legends of Illinois High School Basketball* (Champaign, IL: SportsPublishingLLC.com, 2006).

Bernard, Emily. *Some of My Best Friends: Writings on Interracial Friendship* (New York: Amistad/HarperCollins, 2004).

Billingsley, Andrew. *Black Families in White America* (New York: Simon & Schuster, 1988).

Blum, John Morton. *Years of Discord: American Politics and Society, 1961–1974* (New York: W. W. Norton, 1991).

Bonham, Chad. *Golden Hurricane Basketball at The University of Tulsa* (Charleston, SC: Arcadia, 2004).

Bonilla-Silva, Eduardo. "The Linguistics of Color Blind Racism: How to Talk Nasty About Blacks Without Sounding 'Racist,'" *Critical Sociology*, vol. 28, issues 1–2 (2002), pp. 41–64.

Bowen, William G. et al. *Reclaiming the Game: College Sports and Educational Values* (Princeton, NJ: Princeton University Press, 2003).

Boyd, Todd. *Out of Bounds: Sports, Media, and the Politics of Identity* (Bloomington, IN: Indiana University Press, 1997).

Branch, Taylor. *Parting the Waters: America in the King Years, 1954–1963* (New York: Simon and Schuster, 1988).

_____. *Pillar of Fire: America in the King Years, 1963–1965* (New York: Simon & Schuster, 1998).

Brandom, Robert. *Making It Explicit: Reasoning, Representing, and Discursive Commitment* (Cambridge, MA: Harvard University Press, 1994).

Brehm, Sharon S. and Jack W. Brehm. *Psychological Reactance: A Theory of Freedom and Control* (New York: Academic Press, 1981).

Brick, Howard. *Age of Contradiction: American Thought and Culture in the 1960's* (New York: Twayne Publishers, 1998).

Brown, Judith Olans et al. "Treating Blacks As If They Were White: Problems of Definition and Proof in Section 1982 Cases," *University of Pennsylvania Law Review*, vol. 124, no. 1 (November 1975), pp. 1–44.

Brown, Michael K. et al. *Whitewashing Race: The Myth of a Color-Blind Society* (Berkeley, CA: University of California Press, 2003).

Bunge, Mario. "How Does It Work? The Search for Explanatory Mechanisms," *Philosophy of the Social Sciences*, vol. 34, no. 2 (June 2004), pp. 182–210.

Burns, Stewart. *Social Movements of the 1960's: Searching for Democracy* (Boston: Twayne Publishers, 1990).

Bush, Rod. *We Are Not What We Seem: Black Nationalism and Class Struggle in the American Century* (New York: New York University Press, 1999).

Camp, Elisabeth Maura. *Saying and Seeing As: The Linguistic Uses and Cognitive Effects of Metaphor* (Ph.D. dissertation, University of California, Berkeley, 2003).

Campbell, Nelson, ed. *ILLINKY: High School Basketball in Illinois, Indiana, and Kentucky* (Lexington, MA: S. Greene Press/Pelham Books, 1990).

Carr, Leslie G. *'Color-blind' Racism* (Thousand Oaks, CA: Sage Publications, 1997).

Carson, Clayborne. *In Struggle: SNCC and the Black Awakening of the 1960's* (Cambridge, MA: Harvard University Press, 1995).

Carter, Gregg Lee. "The 1960's Black Riots Revisited: City Level Explanations of Their Severity," *Sociological Inquiry*, vol. 56, no. 2 (Spring 1986), pp. 210–228.

Cashin, Sheryll. *The Failures of Integration: How Race and Class Are Undermining the American Dream* (New York: Public Affairs, 2004).

Chalmers, David Mark. *And the Crooked Places Made Straight: The Struggle for Social Change in the 1960's* (Baltimore: Johns Hopkins University Press, 1996).

Chappell, David L. *Inside Agitators: White Southerners in the Civil Rights Movement* (Baltimore: Johns Hopkins University Press, 1994).

Clinton, William Jefferson. "Erasing America's Color Lines," *New York Times*, January 14, 2001, sec. 4, p. 17.

Cobb, James C. *The Selling of the South: The Southern Crusade for Industrial Development, 1936–1990* (Urbana, IL: University of Illinois Press, 1993).

Coleman, Jonathan. *Long Way to Go: Black and White in America* (New York: Atlantic Monthly Press, 1997).

Collier, Peter and David Horowitz. *Destructive Generation: Second Thoughts About the Sixties* (New York: Summit Books, 1989).

Conley, Dalton. *Honkey* (Berkeley, CA: University of California Press, 2000).

Cose, Ellis. *Color-Blind: Seeing Beyond Race in a Race-Obsessed World* (New York: HarperCollins Publishers, 1997).

Dalton, Harlon L. *Racial Healing: Confronting the Fear Between Blacks and Whites* (New York: Doubleday, 1995).

Daniel, Pete. *The Shadow of Slavery: Peonage in the South, 1901–1969* (Urbana, IL: University of Illinois, 1972).

Darder, Antonia and Rodolfo D. Torres. *After Race: Racism After Multiculturalism* (New York: New York University Press, 2004).

Davis, Abraham L. "The Role of Black Colleges and Black Law Schools in the Training of Black Lawyers and Judges: 1960–1980," *Journal of Negro History*, vol. 70, nos. 1 and 2 (Winter/Spring 1985), pp. 24–34.

Davis, F. James. *Who is Black? One Nation's Definition* (University Park, PA: Pennsylvania State University Press, 2001).

Deford, Frank. "The Negro Is Invited Home," *Sports Illustrated*, June 14, 1965, pp. 26–27.

Dickerson, Debra J. *The End of Blackness: Returning the Souls of Black Folk to Their Rightful Owners* (New York: Pantheon Books, 2004).

Doane, Ashley "Woody" and Eduardo Bonilla-Silva. *White Out: The Continuing Significance of Racism* (New York: Routledge, 2003).

Drake, St. Clair and Horace R. Cayton. *Black Metropolis: A Study of Negro Life in a Northern City* (Chicago: University of Chicago, 1993).

Dreyfuss, Joel. "White Men on Black Power," *Essence*, November 1992, pp. 66–70, 124, 126, 128.

Dyer, Richard. *The Matter of Images: Essays on Representation* (London/New York: Routledge, 2002).

Early, Gerald, ed. *Lure and Loathing: Essays on Race, Identity, and the Ambivalence of Assimilation* (New York: Allen Lane/Penguin Press, 1993).

Edley, Christopher F. *Not All Black and White: Affirmative Action, Race, and American Values* (New York: Hill and Wang, 1996).

Egerton, John. *Speak Now Against the Day: The Generation Before the Civil Rights Movement in the South* (New York: Knopf, 1994).

Entine, Jon. *Taboo: Why Black Athletes Dominate Sports and Why We're Afraid to Talk About It* (New York: Public Affairs, 2000).

Entman, Robert M. and Andrew Rojecki. *The Black Image in the White Mind: Media and Race in America* (Chicago: University of Chicago Press, 2000).

Estes, Stephen Sandford, Jr. *'I Am a Man!' Race, Manhood, and the Struggle for Civil Rights* (Ph.D. dissertation, University of North Carolina, Chapel Hill, 2001).

Farber, David. *The Age of Great Dreams: America in the 1960's* (New York: Hill and Wang, 1994).

Farrell, James J. *The Spirit of the Sixties: Making Postwar Radicalism* [American Radicals Series] (New York: Routledge Press, 1997).

Feagin, Joe R. and Eileen O'Brien. *White Men on Race: Power, Privilege, and The Shaping of Cultural Consciousness* (Boston: Beacon Press, 2003).

Fine, Michelle. *Off-White: Readings on Race, Power, and Society* (New York: Routledge, 1997).

Fischer, Claude S. "The Public and Private Worlds of City Life," *American Sociological Review*, vol. 46, no. 3 (June 1981), pp. 306–316.

Fisher, Anthony Leroy. "The Best Way Out of the Ghetto," *Phi Delta Kappan*, vol. 60, no. 3 (November 1978), p. 240.

Floriani, Ray. *The National Invitation Tournament* (Charleston, SC: Arcadia, 2005).

Fogel, Robert William. *The Slavery Debates, 1952–1990: A Retrospective* (Baton Rouge, LA: Louisiana State University, 2003).

Ford, Richard Thompson. "*Brown*'s Ghost," *Harvard Law Review*, vol. 117, no. 5 (March 2004), pp. 1305–1333.

Foster, Hal, ed. *Vision and Visuality* (Seattle: Bay Press, 1988).

Franklin, John Hope. *Racial Equality in America* (Chicago: University of Chicago Press, 1976).

Frazier, John W. *Race and Place: Equity Issues in Urban America* (Boulder, CO: Westview Press, 2003).

Fredrickson, George M. *Racism: A Short History* (Princeton, NJ: Princeton University Press, 2002).

Frey, Darcy. *The Last Shot: City Streets, Basketball Dreams* (Boston: Houghton Mifflin Co., 1994).

Gaines, Kevin K. *Uplifting the Race: Black Leadership, Politics, and Culture in the Twentieth Century* (Chapel Hill, NC: University of North Carolina Press, 1996).

Gates, Henry Louis. *America Behind the Color Line: Dialogues With African Americans* (New York: Warner Books, 2004).

Gems, Gerald. "Blocked Shot: The Development of Basketball in the African-American Community of Chicago," *Journal of Sport History*, vol. 22, no. 2 (Summer 1995), pp. 135–148.

Gentile, Derek. *Smooth Moves: The Evolution of Basketball and the Plays and Players Who Made It Great* (New York: Black Dog & Leventhal Publishers, Inc., 2003).

George, Nelson. *Elevating the Game: Black Men and Basketball.* (New York: HarperCollins, 1992).

Gerson, Mark. "Black Kids and Basketball," *Commentary*, vol. 99, no. 3 (March 1995), pp. 56–58.

Gitlin, Todd. *The Sixties: Years of Hope, Days of Rage* (New York: Bantam Books, 1993).

Goffman, Erving. *The Presentation of Self in Everyday Life* (Woodstock, NY: Overlook Press, 1973).

Goldfield, David R. *Black, White and Southern Culture* (Baton Rouge, LA: Louisiana State University Press, 1990).

Gordy (A Division of Motown Record Corp.), *The Great March on Washington* (no. 908), 1963.

Grace, Kevin. *Cincinnati Hoops* (Charleston, SC: Arcadia, 2003).

Graves, Joseph L., Jr. *The Race Myth: Why We Pretend Race Exists in America* (New York: Dutton, 2004).

Grossman, James R. *Land of Hope: Chicago, Black Southerners, and the Great Migration* (Chicago: University of Chicago Press, 1989).

Halberstam, David. *The Breaks of the Game* (New York: Knopf, 1981).

Hall, Edward T. *The Silent Language* (Garden City, NY: Anchor Books, 1973).

Hall, Ronald. E. "Clowns, Buffoons, and Gladiators: Media Portrayals of African-American Men," *Journal of Men's Studies*, vol. 1, no. 3 (February 1993), pp. 239–251.

Haney-López, Ian. *White By Law: The Legal Construction of Race* (New York: New York University Press, 1996).

Harvey, James C. *Black Civil Rights During the Johnson Administration* (Jackson, MS: University and College Press of Mississippi, 1973).

Hayduk, Leslie A. "Personal Space: Understanding the Simplex Model," *Journal of Nonverbal Behavior*, vol. 18, no. 3 (Fall 1994), pp. 245–260.

Healey, Joseph F., ed. *Race, Ethnicity, Gender, and Class: The Sociology of Group Conflict and Change* (Thousand Oaks, CA: Pine Forge Press, 2003).

Heller, Morton A. and Soledad Ballesteros, eds. *Touch and Blindness: Psychology and Neuroscience* (Mahwah, NJ: Lawrence Erlbaum Associates, 2006).

Henderson-King, Eaaron I. and Richard E. Nisbett. "Anti-Black Prejudice as a Function of Exposure to the Negative Behavior of a Single Black Person," *Journal of Personality and Social Psychology*, vol. 71, no. 4 (October 1996), pp. 654–664.

Hersch, Joni. "Skin-Tone Effects among African Americans: Perceptions and Reality," *American Economic Review*, vol. 96, no. 2 (May 2006), pp. 251–255.

Hight, Marc A. "Why We Do Not See What We Feel," *Pacific Philosophical Quarterly*, vol. 83, no. 2 (June 2002), pp. 148–162.

Hijaya, James A. "The Conservative 1960's," *Journal of American Studies*, vol. 37, no. 2 (August 2003), pp. 201–227.

Hill, Mark E. "Race of the Interviewer and Perception of Skin Color: Evidence from the Multi-City Study of Urban Inequality," *American Sociological Review*, vol. 67, no. 1 (February 2002), pp. 99–108.

Hill, Renée A. "Seeing Clearly Without Being Blinded: Obstacles to Black Self-Examination," *Journal of Negro Education*, vol. 72, no. 2 (Spring 2003), pp. 208–216.

Holland, Jerold W. *Black Recreation: A Historical Perspective* (Chicago: Burnham Inc., 2002).

Horton, James Oliver. *Free People of Color: Inside the African American Community* (Washington, DC: Smithsonian Institution Press, 1993).

Howard, Gary R. *We Can't Teach What We Don't Know: White Teachers, Multiracial Schools* (New York: Teachers College Press, 1999).

Hudson, J. Blaine. "Affirmative Action and American Racism in Historical Perspective," *Journal of Negro History*, vol. 84, no. 3 (Summer 1999), pp. 260–274.

Hunter, Andrea G. and James Earl Davis, "Hidden Voices of Black Men: The Meaning, Structure, and Complexity of Manhood," *Journal of Black Studies*, vol. 25, no. 1 (September 1994), pp. 20–40.

Issel, William. *Social Change in the United States, 1945–1983* (New York: Schocken Books, 1987).

Isserman, Maurice and Michael Kazin. *America Divided: The Civil War of the 1960's* (New York: Oxford University Press, 2004).

Jackson, Derrick Z. "Invisible or Thugs: The Stereotyping of Black Males," *Chicago Tribune*, June 6, 2005, p. 17.

Jenkins, J. Craig et al. "Political Opportunities and African-American Protest, 1948–1997," *American Journal of Sociology*, vol. 109, no. 2 (September 2003), pp. 277–303.

Jordan, Larry E. "Folks Won't Turn Out to See Grambling Play: An Examination of Opportunity and Adaptation in Athletics," *Journal of Popular Culture*, vol. 13, no. 3 (Spring 1980), pp. 447–460.

Katz, Milton S. "Coach John B. McLendon, Jr. and the Integration of Intercollegiate and Professional Athletics in Post World War II America," *Journal of American Culture*, vol. 13, no. 4 (1990), pp. 35–39.

Katznelson, Ira. *When Affirmative Action Was White: An Untold History of Racial Inequality in Twentieth-Century America* (New York: W. W. Norton & Company, 2005).

Kean, Melissa Fitzsimmons. *'At a Most Uncomfortable Speed': The Desegregation of the South's Private Universities, 1945–1964* (Ph.D. dissertation, Rice University, Houston, 2000).

Keller, Evelyn Fox and Christine R. Grontkowski, "The Mind's Eye," in Sandra Harding and Merrill B. Hintikka, eds., *Discovering Reality: Feminist Perspectives on Epistemology, Metaphysics, Methodology, and Philosophy of Science* (Dordrecht/Boston: D. Reidel, 1983).

King, C. Richard. *Beyond the Cheers: Race as Spectacle in College Sport* (Albany, NY: State University of New York Press, 2001).

Kirkpatrick, Curry. "The Night They Drove Old Dixie Down," *Sports Illustrated*, April 1, 1991, pp. 70–79, 81.

Kittay, Eva Feder. *Metaphor: Its Cognitive Force and Linguistic Structure* (New York: Oxford University Press, 1987).

Kivel, Paul. *Uprooting Racism: How White People Can Work for Racial Justice* (Gabriola Island, BC: New Society Publishers, 2002).

Klarman, Michael J. "How *Brown* Changed Race Relations: The Backlash Thesis," *Journal of American History*, vol. 81, no. 1 (June 1994), pp. 81–118.

Klatch, Rebecca E. *A Generation Divided: The New Left, the New Right and the 1960's* (Berkeley, CA: University of California Press, 1999).

Kluger, Richard. *Simple Justice: The History of* Brown v. Board of Education *and Black America's Struggle for Equality* (New York: Knopf, 2004).

Kotz, Nick. *Judgment Days: Lyndon Baines Johnson, Martin Luther King, Jr., and the Laws That Changed America* (Boston: Houghton Mifflin, 2005).

Kroeger, Brooke. *Passing: When People Can't Be Who They Are* (New York: Public Affairs, 2003).

Kull, Andrew. *The Color-Blind Constitution* (Cambridge, MA: Harvard University Press, 1992).

Lakoff, George and Mark Turner. *More Than Cool Reason: A Field Guide to Poetic Metaphor* (Chicago: University of Chicago Press, 1989).

Lau, Richard R. and Dan Russell. "Attributions in the Sports Pages," *Journal of Personality and Social Psychology*, vol. 39, no. 1 (July 1980), pp. 29–38.

Lawson, Steven F. *Black Ballots: Voting Rights in the South, 1944–1969* (New York: Columbia University Press, 1976).

Lee, Cynthia Kwei Yung. "Race and Self-Defense: Toward a Normative Conception of Reasonableness," *Minnesota Law Review*, vol. 81, no. 2 (December 1996), pp. 367–500.

Lee, James Kyung-Jin. *Urban Triage: Race and the Fictions of Multiculturalism* (Minneapolis: University of Minnesota Press, 2004).

Leiserson, Avery. *The American South in the 1960's* (New York: Praeger, 1964).

Lemann, Nicholas. *The Promised Land: The Great Black Migration and How It Changed America* (New York: A. A. Knopf, 1991).

Leu, Bob (with Henry Jacobs). *Good Evening, Bradley Basketball Fans: The Story of the 'Famous Five' and a History of Bradley Basketball* (Peoria, IL: Walfred, 1976).

Loury, Glenn C. *The Anatomy of Racial Inequality* (Cambridge, MA: Harvard University Press, 2002).

Macedo, Donaldo. *Literacies of Power: What Americans Are Not Allowed to Know* (Boulder, CO: Westview Press, 1994).

Malcomson, Scott L. *One Drop of Blood: The American Misadventure of Race* (New York: Farrar, Straus Giroux, 2000).

Malik, Kenan. *The Meaning of Race: Race, History, and Culture in Western Society* (New York: New York University Press, 1996).

Marable, Manning. *Beyond Black and White: Transforming African-American Politics* (London/New York: Verso, 1995).

Markides, Kyriacos C. and Steven F. Cohn. "External Conflict/Internal Cohesion: A Reevaluation of an Old Theory," *American Sociological Review*, vol. 47, no. 1 (February 1982), pp. 88–98.

Marks, Jonathan. "A Feckless Quest for the Basketball Gene," *New York Times*, April 8, 2000, p. A13.

Mathis, Deborah. *Yet a Stranger: Why Black Americans Still Don't Feel at Home* (New York: Warner Books, 2002).

McCormick, Robert A. and Amy Christian McCormick. "The Myth of the Student-Athlete: The College Athlete as Employee," *Washington Law Review*, vol. 81, no. 1 (February 2006), pp. 71–157.

McKee, James B. *Sociology and the Race Problem: The Failure of a Perspective* (Urbana, IL: University of Illinois Press, 1993).

McPherson Lionel K. and Tommie Shelby. "Blackness and Blood: Interpreting African American Identity," *Philosophy & Public Affairs*, vol. 32, no. 2 (Spring 2004), pp. 171–192.

McQuaid, Kim. *The Anxious Years: America in the Vietnam-Watergate Era* (New York: Basic Books, 1989).

McWhorter, John. *Winning the Race: Beyond the Crisis in Black America* (New York: Gotham Books, 2006).

McWilliams, John C. *The 1960's Cultural Revolution* (Westport, CT: Greenwood Press, 2000).

Meyer, Stephen Grant. *As Long As They Don't Move Next Door: Segregation and Racial Conflict in American Neighborhoods* (Lanham, MD: Rowman & Littlefield, 2000).

Mills, Charles W. *Blackness Visible: Essays on Philosophy and Race* (Ithaca, NY: Cornell University Press, 1998).

Minow, Martha. *Making All the Difference: Inclusion, Exclusion, and American Law* (Ithaca, NY: Cornell University Press, 1990).

Moore, Elizabeth R. "Being and Blackness: The Existential Legacy in African-American Thought," *Review of Existential Psychology & Psychiatry*, vol. 26, nos. 2&3 (2001), pp. 147–162.

Murphree, Vanessa D. "'Black Power': Public Relations and Social Change in the 1960's," *American Journalism*, vol. 21, no. 3 (Summer 2004), pp. 13–32.

Norrell, Robert J. *The House I Live In: Race in the American Century* (New York: Oxford University Press, 2005).

Novick, Michael. *White Lies, White Power: The Fight Against White Supremacy and Reactionary Violence* (Monroe, ME: Common Courage Press, 1995).

O'Brien, Gail Williams. *The Color of the Law: Race, Violence, and Justice in the Post-World War II South* (Chapel Hill, NC: University of North Carolina Press, 1999).

Ogletree, Charles J., Jr. *All Deliberate Speed: Reflections on the First Hall Century of* Brown v. Board of Education (New York: W. W. Norton & Company, 2004).

Oliver, Melvin L. and Thomas M. Shapiro. *Black Wealth, White Wealth: A New Perspective on Racial Inequality* (New York: Routledge, 1995).

Olsen, Jack. "Part 3: The Black Athlete," *Sports Illustrated*, July 15, 1968, pp. 28–43.

Page, Clarence. "'Racial' is Not Always 'Racist'," *Chicago Tribune*, November 6, 2005, sec. 2, p. 11.

Patterson, Orlando. *Rituals of Blood: Consequences of Slavery in Two American Centuries* (Washington, DC: Civitas/ CounterPoint, 1998).

Pattillo-McCoy, Mary. *Black Picket Fences: Privilege and Peril Aming the Black Middle Class* (Chicago: University of Chicago Press, 1999).

Payne, Charles. "Debating the Civil Rights Movement: The View from the Trenches," in Steven F. Lawson and Payne, *Debating the Civil Rights Movement, 1945–1968* (Lanham, MD: Rowman & Littlefield, 1998), pp. 108–111.

Perry, Michael. *Tales from Cincinnati Bearcats Basketball* (Champaign, IL: Sports Publishing L.L.C., 2004).

Postrel, Virginia. "Economic Scene: The Long-term Consequences of the Race Riots in the Late 1960's Come into View," *New York Times*, December 30, 2004, p. C2.

Quarles, Benjamin. *The Negro in the Making of America* (New York: Collier Books/Macmillan Publishing Company, 1987).

Raspberry, William. "Moral Authority, Civil Rights and the '63 March," *Chicago Tribune*, August 31, 1992, p. 9.

Rhoden, William C. "A Conference Too Good for Its Own Good," *New York Times*, March 5, 2006, sec. 8, pp. 1, 3.

Richardson, Steve. *A Century of Sports: Missouri Valley Conference, 1907–2007* (St. Louis: Reedy Press and MathisJones Communications, LLC, 2006).

Riches, William Terence Martin. *The Civil Rights Movement: Struggle and Resistance* (New York: Macmillan, 1997).

Robertson, Oscar. "Putting the 'I' in Lakers," *New York Times*, February 18, 2006, p. A31.

Roediger, David R. *Colored White: Transcending the Racial Past* (Berkeley/London: University of California Press, 2002).

Sack, Allen L. "College Basketball and Role Conflict: A National Survey," *Sociology of Sport Journal*, vol. 2, no. 3 (September 1985), pp. 195–209.

Sailes, Gary A. "An Investigation of Campus Stereotypes: The Myth of Black Athletic Superiority and the Dumb Jock Stereotype," *Sociology of Sport Journal,* vol. 10 (March 1993), pp. 88–97.

Salzberg, Charles. *From Set Shot to Slam Dunk: The Glory Days of Basketball in the Words of Those Who Played It* (New York: E. P. Dutton, 1987).

Samuels, Albert L. *Is Separate Unequal?; Black Colleges and the Challenge to Desegregation* (Lawrence, KS: University Press of Kansas, 2004).

Saul, Scott. *Freedom Is, Freedom Ain't: Jazz and the Making of the Sixties* (Cambridge, MA: Harvard University Press, 2003).

Sewell, Stacy Kinlock. "The 'Not-Buying Power' of the Black Community: Urban Boycotts and Equal Employment Opportunity, 1960–1964," *Journal of African American History,* vol. 89, no. 2 (Spring 2004), pp. 135–151.

Shapiro, Thomas. *The Hidden Cost of Being African-American: How Wealth Perpetuates Inequality* (New York: Oxford University Press, 2004).

Shelby, Tommie. *We Who Are Dark: The Philosophical Foundations of Black Solidarity* (Cambridge, MA: Belknap Press of Harvard University Press, 2005).

Shouler, Kenneth. "The Big O," *Cigar Aficionado* (March-April, 2005), pp. 174, 176, 179, 182.

Silberman, Charles E. *Crisis in Black and White* (New York: Random House, 1964).

Sitkoff, Harvard. *The Struggle for Black Equality, 1954–1980* (New York: Hill and Wang, 1981).

Smith, T. Alexander and Lenahan O'Connell. *Black Anxiety, White Guilt, and the Politics of Status Frustration* (Westport, CT: Praeger, 1997).

Smith-McLallen, Aaron et al. "Black and White: The Role of Color Bias in Implicit Race Bias," *Social Cognition,* vol. 24, no. 1 (February 2006), pp. 46–73.

Spickard, Paul and G. Reginald Daniel, eds. *Racial Thinking in the United States: Uncompleted Independence* (Notre Dame, IN: University of Notre Dame Press, 2004).

Spivey, Donald. "The Black Athlete in Big-Time Intercollegiate Sports, 1941–1968," *Phylon*, vol. 44, no. 2 (June 1983), pp. 116–125.

Steele, Shelby. *White Guilt: How Blacks and Whites Together Destroyed the Promise of the Civil Rights Era* (New York: HarperCollins, 2006).

Steigerwald, David. *The Sixties and the End of Modern America* (New York: St. Martin's Press, 1995).

Steinhorn, Leonard and Barbara Diggs-Brown. *By the Color of Our Skin: The Illusion of Integration and the Reality of Race* (New York: Plume/Penguin Putnam, 1999).

Stewart, John, ed. *Beyond the Symbol Model: Reflections on the Representational Nature of Language* (Albany, NY: State University of New York Press, 1996).

Swidler, Ann. "Culture in Action: Symbols and Strategies," *American Sociological Review*, vol. 51, no. 2 (April 1986), pp. 273–286.

Taguieff, Pierre-André. *The Force of Prejudice: On Racism and Its Doubles* (Minneapolis: University of Minnesota Press, 2001).

Tatum, Beverly Daniel. *'Why Are All the Black Kids Sitting Together in the Cafeteria?' and Other Conversations about Race* (New York: BasicBooks, 1997).

Thompson, Margaret Susan. *The Yoke of Grace* (New York: Oxford University Press, 2003).

Trotter, Joe W., ed. *The Great Migration in Historical Perspective: New Dimensions of Race, Class, and Gender* (Bloomington, IN: Indiana University Press, 1991).

Tucker, Linda. "Blackballed: Basketball and Representation of the Black Male Athlete," *American Behavioral Scientist*, vol. 47, no. 3 (November 2003), pp. 306–328.

Tyson, Timothy B. *Radio Free Dixie: Robert F. Williams & the Roots of Black Power* (Chapel Hill, NC: University of North Carolina Press, 1999).

Vargas, Sylvia R. Lazos. "Deconstructing Homo[geneous] Americanus: The White Ethnic Immigrant Narrative and Its Exclusionary Effect," *Tulane Law Review*, vol. 72, no. 5 (May 1998), pp. 1493–1596.

Wachtel, Paul L. *Race in the Mind of America: Breaking the Vicious Circle Between Blacks and Whites* (New York: Routledge, 1999).

Walker, Anders. *The Ghost of Jim Crow: Law, Culture, and the Subversion of Civil Rights, 1954–1965* (Ph.D. dissertation, Yale University, New Haven, 2003).

Webb, Clive. "'A Cheap Trafficking in Human Misery': The Reverse Freedom Rides of 1962," *Journal of American Studies*, vol. 38, no. 2 (August 2004), pp. 249–271.

Wellman, David T. *Portraits of White Racism* (New York: Cambridge University Press, 1993).

West, Cornel. *Race Matters* (Boston: Beacon Press, 1993).

Wiggins, David K. "'Great Speed But Little Stamina': The Historical Debate over Black Athletic Superiority," *Journal of Sport History*, vol. 16, no. 2 (Summer 1989), pp. 158–185.

_____, ed. *Out of the Shadows: A Biographical History of African American Athlete*s (Fayetteville, AR: University of Arkansas Press, 2006).

Wilkinson, J. Harvie. *From* Brown to Bakke*: The Supreme Court and School Integration, 1954–1978* (New York: Oxford University Press, 1979).

Williams, Juan. *Eyes on the Prize: America's Civil Rights Years, 1954–1965* (New York: Viking Penguin, 1987).

Williams, Lea Esther. *Servants of the People: The 1960's Legacy of African-American Leadership* (New York: St. Martin's Griffin, 1998).

Wilson, William Julius et al., eds. *America Becoming: Racial Trends and Their Consequences* (Washington, DC: National Academy Press, 2001).

Wolff, Alexander. *Basketball: A History of the Game* (New York: Bishop Books, 1997).

Woodiwiss, Anthony. *The Visual in Social Theory* (London/New York: Athlone Press, 2001).

Woodward, C. Vann. *The Strange Career of Jim Crow* (New York: Oxford University Press, 1966).

Wynter, Leon E. *American Skin: Pop Culture, Big Business, and the End of White America* (New York: Crown Publishers, 2002).

Yetman, Norman R. et al. "Racial Participation and Integration in Intercollegiate Basketball, 1958–1980," *Journal of Sport Behavior*, vol. 5, no. 1 (March 1982), pp. 44–56.